FESTIVE AS F*CK

FESTIVE AS F✱CK

Hilariously Irreverent Cross-Stitch for the Holidays

weldon**owen**

CONTENTS

IT'S THE MOST WONDERFUL F&#K%*G TIME OF THE YEAR!

The holidays can be a whole lot of fun—who doesn't love the food, the parties, the movies, and the presents! But for those of us with irreverent hearts and snarky senses of humor, sometimes all of that "Ho Ho Ho" and "Happy Holidays" and Dean Martin crooning about marshmallow worlds can get as sticky-sweet as a piece of grandma's ribbon candy.

If you've landed on the Naughty list more times than the Nice, are drawn to the Heat Miser, or chuckle with glee at Clark Griswold kicking the crud out of those plastic reindeer, this is the book for you! This holly jolly collection, created by some of today's most inventive and talented cross-stitch artists, features hilarious holiday-themed cross-stitch projects for all skill levels and all levels of bawdiness. You can show off your festively snarky side with the "Hallelujah, Holy Shit, Where's the Tylenol" sampler (p. 98), warn your siblings not to pull their shenanigans with "Deck the Halls and Not Your Family" (p. 42), let kids know that tattling about presents is not cool (p. 72), or announce to the world that you are the OG when it comes to wrapping presents (p. 50).

If you're going crazy trying to find the perfect gift to make for your nearest and dearest, don't get your tinsel in a tangle—we've got you covered. Stitch a little "Merry Drunk, I'm Christmas" (p. 36) for that friend who loves their holiday spirits; make up a quick "Ho" ornament (p. 22) for a last-minute hostess gift; or let your bestie with the wicked sense of humor know how much you like their balls (p. 46)!

Whether you're looking to just stab your holiday stress away, deck your halls with a little sauciness, or stitch the perfect irreverent gift, we hope this book will help you handle the holidays with a little snark and a lot of laughs. Happy fucking holidays!

THE BASICS

WHAT IN THE HELL DO I NEED?

Luckily, you don't have to break the bank to start cross-stitching. A hoop, some floss (yarn), fabric, and a needle are all you need. You can get super-fancy and buy all kinds of accessories, but don't feel you have to—a pair of regular scissors will cut floss just as well as those gorgeous little embroidery scissors! So, let's talk about the basics:

The Fabric

Technically, cross-stitch can be done on any kind of fabric, but for this book we are only using Aida cloth. Aida is a cloth that is made specifically for cross-stitch and is woven in such a way that it looks like a grid with holes at even intervals, so you know exactly where your needle goes.

Aida cloth comes in an array of colors, so don't think you always have to use white. Aida also comes in precut sizes as well as rolls that you can cut down; if you're planning on doing more than one piece, your best bet is to buy the roll.

Aida cloth comes in different "counts"—the count refers to the number of holes (or stitches) per inch (2.5 cm) of fabric. The easiest to use is 14-count Aida—meaning 14 stitches to the inch (2.5 cm). The higher the count, the tighter the stitches will be, and the smaller the final piece will be (and the more challenging it can be to stitch). Unless you need to fit a specific frame (or want a challenge!), we suggest sticking to 14-count Aida, but in case you do want to play with the size, each pattern gives you the final piece size in different cloth counts.

The Floss

Cross-stitch is done with cotton embroidery floss, which is made up of six thin strands twisted together. There are several brands, but for this book we are using DMC, which is the most common and accessible brand. For almost all of the patterns in this book you will use two strands, but in general, the cloth count determines how many of the six strands you will use:

11-count: three strands
12-count: two or three strands
14-count: two strands
16-count: two strands
18-count: one or two strands
20-count: one strand

MAKE IT BOLD

If you prefer a denser look to your finished work (so that the Xs look more like full blocks of color), use three strands of floss on 14-count Aida. Don't go any higher, though—your piece will start to look clunky and stitching will be difficult. Remember that if you do go up to three strands, you will have to increase the amount of floss needed for the project.

The Needle

Because Aida cloth already has the holes in it, a tapestry needle is best to use, as it has a blunt tip. Tapestry needles come in a variety of sizes, and you want to make sure you don't get too large of a size—it will stretch the holes in your cloth and distort your project. For 14-count Aida, we recommend using a size 24 tapestry needle.

The Hoop

You always want to work your cross-stitch on a hoop; this keeps the fabric tight and your stitches neat and uniform. People have their preferences when it comes to the size hoop to use. Some prefer to work the pattern in sections, using smaller hoops that are easier to hold in your hand; others prefer to be able to have the entire pattern visible in the hoop. The choice is yours. There are also several kinds of frames—plastic, wood, screw frames, snap frames—but the most common and easiest to find are plastic and wood. Plastic tends to hold the fabric better, but the wood can go from working hoop to display hoop easily.

A WORD ABOUT SCISSORS

Like we said at the beginning, you don't *need* a special pair of scissors for cross-stitch—really, any scissors will do. However, a small pair of embroidery scissors does have one distinct advantage—their small, sharp points come in handy if you screw up and need to pull out stitches.

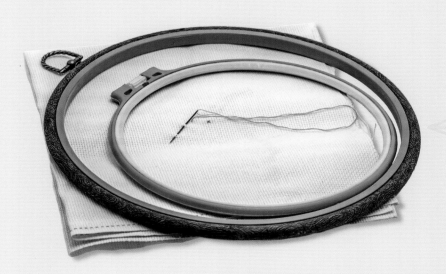

THE SeTUP

Before we dive into stitching, let's get our cloth and thread ready.

Cutting the Cloth

Let's face it, mistakes happen in cross-stitch—miscounting stitches, not having enough thread—and all of them can be fixed, except one: running out of fabric. There is no coming back from cutting your fabric too small and running out of room for the pattern! It's always best to leave yourself a healthy border of at least 3 to 4 inches (7.5 to 10 cm) on each side. So, if your finished piece is 4 x 6 inches (10 x 15 cm), your piece of fabric should be at least 10 x 12 inches (25 x 30.5 cm). This may seem like a lot, but it's better to have excess than to run out! (It will also help when it comes time to mount your piece.) Each pattern in this book will give you the size cloth you need, including the border, in addition to the dimensions of the finished piece.

Finding the Center

It's always best to start stitching in the middle of the pattern; if you start in a corner and misjudge the placement, you could run out of fabric!

Finding the middle of your piece of cloth is easy: Just fold it in half lengthwise, then in half widthwise and press the folds with your finger. Open the fabric, and where the two creases intersect is your center. Insert your needle into this intersection so you won't lose your place when you pull the fabric taut in your hoop.

Getting It On (the Hoop)

Hoops have two parts—the inner (smaller) and outer (larger) hoop. On some hoops, the inner has a little lip that you can feel, which helps the fabric stay in place. If yours has that lip, that lip faces up. Place the inner hoop on a flat surface, then lay the fabric on top (that lip should now be against the fabric). Center the fabric, using the marked center as a guide. The outer hoop has a screw and nut at the top; unscrew it as far as you can without the nut falling off, then carefully place it on top of the fabric. Push it down until the two hoops meet and the fabric is taut. Tighten the screw just enough to hold the fabric, then pull the edges of the fabric to make it as tight as you want. (Some people like a little give, others like it as tight as a drum—it's up to you). Once the fabric is taut, tighten the screw all the way.

Floss That Needle

Before threading the needle, we have to get the floss ready. Cut a piece of floss about the length of your forearm (from the tip of your middle finger to the crook of your arm). If you make it any longer you'll risk it tangling and knotting while you stitch, which is a bitch, to say the least. Take one end and hold it between your thumb and first finger. Rub it a little bit to separate the strands, then take two strands in one hand and the four in the other and slowly pull them apart. Set aside the four strands and thread your needle with the two. We're ready to go!

GETTING THIS MERRY SHOW ON THE ROAD

Cross-stitch couldn't be simpler—it is just making a series of Xs, which is made up of two small stitches that cross diagonally. The Aida cloth makes it even simpler, by showing you exactly where your needle should go, so there is no guesswork! But before we get to the stitches, a word about the pattern.

How to Read the Pattern

The patterns in this book are what is called *counted* cross-stitch. It is called that because you literally count the number of colored blocks on the pattern and stitch that number. To some it may sound tedious, or intimidating, but it's actually much easier than working on a printed pattern, as sometimes the printing isn't done well or the pattern is printed crooked on the fabric, which makes figuring out where colors begin and end a disaster. In counted cross-stitch, there is no guessing—if you have five red blocks, you make five red stitches. Easy peasy.

A cross-stitch pattern is made up of colored blocks on a grid (just like the grid of the Aida cloth). Each block on the grid represents one X of cross-stitch. The colors correspond to the color chart, which tells you which color of floss to use. Some patterns that have several colors also include symbols in the colored blocks to make it even easier to determine which color you should use.

A couple of specifics on the patterns:

1. On each pattern you'll see two red lines running through them—one vertical and one horizontal. These are to help you determine the center of your pattern—where they intersect is the center.

2. The grids have darker lines at every ten stitches, to help you with counting larger numbers of stitches.

BREAKING UP THE PATTERN

We have spread out the larger patterns over a couple of pages, in order to make the pattern easier to read. To help navigate between pages, a repeat of five rows from the previous page is shown in gray—*do not stitch* the grayed-out section; it is only there for reference!

Where to Start

Don't listen to that singing nun—the best place to start a cross-stitch project is in the middle, so that the pattern is centered on the canvas. But again, this is personal preference—if working from the center completely stresses you out, you can start from any point in the pattern. Just count the number of stitches (blocks) from the center of the pattern (the intersection of the red lines) to the point you want to stitch, then count the same number of squares on your fabric, using the center you've marked as the reference.

To Knot or Not to Knot

There are some cross-stitchers who will tell you to never knot your floss, and there are some reasons for not knotting. But what it really comes down to is this: how much you care about the back of your piece. Some people insist that the back of a piece has to look as pristine as the front, but honestly, who is ever going to see the back? Don't let the back of your piece stress you out; if you're a beginner, or just don't give a jingle jangle about the back (and why should you?), go ahead and knot your floss. Just simply tie a small knot in the end of your thread.

(One note: If you are planning to display your piece in a frame, it is best not to use knots, as they will leave lumps when mounted on the frame board. If you're displaying the piece in a hoop, you won't have to mount the piece on a board, and knots will work just fine.)

If you want go no-knot, when you pull your thread through the first hole, hold about 1 inch (2.5 cm) of thread on the back side with your finger. Keep holding it while you stitch the next few stitches over that thread. (This is called *anchoring* the thread.)

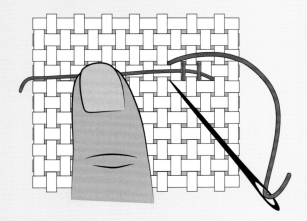

No matter whether you use a knot or anchor, when you are finished with that thread, turn your piece over and work your needle under a couple of stitches, pull the thread through, and cut.

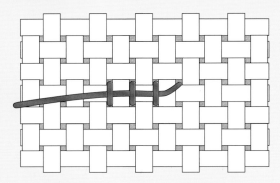

THE KNOTLESS LOOP

This is a neat and super-easy way to avoid a knot, if you're using two strands of floss. Cut a piece of floss twice the length you need, then only pull out a single strand instead of two. Bring the two ends of the single strand together, so you have a loop at the other end. Thread the side with the ends through the needle. Come up through the fabric for your first stitch, leaving the loop in back, then come back down and thread the needle through the loop. Gently pull until the loop flattens at the back.

THE STITCHES

Okay, now that we're all ready with the fabric and needle, and know how to read the pattern, it's time to learn how to do the stitches.

Single Cross-Stitch

It couldn't be easier.

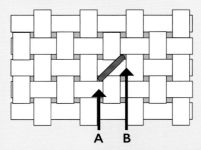

1. Make the first part of your X (/) by bringing your needle from the back through one hole (A). This will be the lower-left corner of your stitch. Pull your thread all the way through.

2. Insert your needle through the hole that is diagonally to the right (B), and pull the thread through. You should now have a diagonal stitch—the first part of your cross.

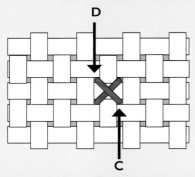

3. Now bring your needle up through the lower-right corner hole (C), and then down through the upper-left corner hole (D). That's it!

Multiple Cross-Stitches

If you have a number of the same color stitches to do, you can work all of the first diagonals together (/////) and then go back and work the second diagonal (\\\\\) together. To do this:

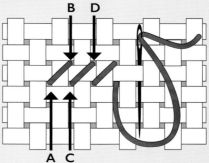

1. Come up through the bottom-left hole of the first stitch (A), go down into the top-right hole (B), come up again in the next bottom-right hole (C) (which is now the beginning of your next diagonal stitch) and then down into the next top-right hole (D).

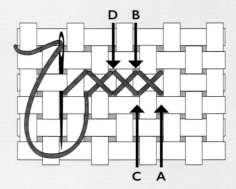

2. Repeat until you get to the end, then work back across the row to complete the stitches in the other direction.

This technique is also really handy when it comes to large sections of color—and can save lots of miscounting headaches. Stitch just the outline of a large color section with the first diagonal, then go back and fill in. This way, if you do miscount the outline, you're only pulling out a handful of single stitches!

The Backstitch

Technically embroidery, the backstitch gives you a nice, unbroken line, which can look pretty against all of those Xs! (See the "Fancy Holiday Anxiety" pattern on 28). It's just as easy as the cross-stitch:

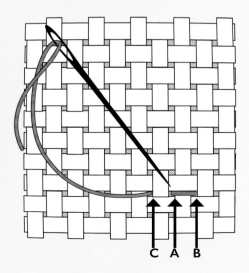

C A B

1. Bring your needle up from back to front (we'll call this A). Take your needle down into the hole to the horizontal right (this is B). This is one stitch.

2. For your second stitch, come up in the hole to the left of A (this is C), then back down into the hole of A. This is the *back* part of backstitch.

3. To make the next stitch, come up in the hole to the left of C, then down into C; continue to come up through the hole to the left in the line, and go down into the hole of the previous stitch. You should now have a straight line!

The French Knot

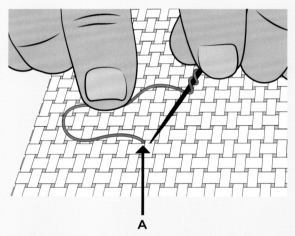

A

1. On the back of your project, secure your thread by running it under several stitches (you can knot it, but if you are mounting your piece in a frame, that knot could create a bump under your project).

2. Instead of coming up in a premade hole, you're going to come up in the middle of a square—this will help secure the thread. Bring your needle up through the middle of a square, and pull the thread all the way through (making sure not to pull it out from the anchoring on the back). This is A on the diagram.

3. Now, rest your hoop on your lap or on the table. You're going to need both hands on top of the project for this next part.

4. With one hand, hold the thread taut, about an inch (2.5 cm) or so away from the fabric. With your other hand, bring your needle right next to the thread, and wind the thread around the needle twice, from front to back. Gently pull the thread to keep it taut.

5. Keeping that thread taut, push the tip of your needle into the fabric right next to point A (don't pull it all the way through yet). Again, keeping the thread taut, push the loops on the needle down so that they are resting on the fabric.

6. Take your needle hand under the hoop, and gently pull the needle and thread through. Keep holding that thread on top taut with the other hand until the needle is all the way through, then use your thumbnail to hold the thread down until it is completely pulled through.

Carrying the Thread

You've got little bits of green all over the pattern—do you have to cut the thread and restart for every section?

Not necessarily. If the sections are in close proximity, you can do what is called *carrying the thread* (which just means not cutting the thread between the sections). You only want to do this over three or four blank squares at most—any more, and that carried thread can start showing through the holes in the fabric. If you're carrying across an area that's already stitched, you can go a little farther, but just weave your needle under the stitched section, to tack down that carried thread.

HO HO HOLY SH✱T!

Fixing a Miscount

Miscounting stitches happens to everyone, no matter how experienced you are. It's just a fact of cross-stitch life! There is nothing worse than getting halfway through a pattern and realizing that two sections aren't matching up. The best advice is (to paraphrase the old carpenter's saying): count twice, stitch once. Stop occasionally and just do a quick check to make sure everything is lining up on the fabric as it is in the pattern. Better to find out sooner rather than later!

Don't stress if you've miscounted; the mistake is easily fixable. Just take your needle and pick out the erroneous stitches. If it's a section that's already been completed, use a seam ripper or to tip of your embroidery scissors to clip out a few stitches (always working from the back), and then pick out the rest with your needle.

But most importantly, don't beat yourself up or get stressed. It's all part of the process!

Out, Out, Damned Spot!

No matter how careful you are, your project can get soiled. No worries here, though—you can wash your piece! Just place it in a bath of tepid water mixed with a mild laundry detergent, swish it around (don't rub or twist the fabric), and let it set. Then rinse (don't wring it out), lay it flat on a bath towel, and roll up the towel to squeeze out the excess water. Lay flat to dry.

Washing your piece is also great for getting out the circles that your hoop leaves in the cloth!

I'M DONE STABBING. NOW WHAT DO I DO?

Now that you've stabbed away all your aggression, it's time to show off your piece. There are lots of ways you can do it, all of which are pretty easy. But first, you have to get the piece ready for framing.

Prepping Your Piece

Before you frame, you might want to wash your fabric (see page 15). Not only will this get the fabric clean, but it will also remove the indents left by the hoop. Whether you wash the fabric or not, you're definitely going to need to iron it. Put a clean, white dish towel down on your ironing board. Lay the piece face-down and place another dish towel on top. With your iron set on steam, slowly press the piece until the creases are gone.

Hooping Your Piece

For this, you'll need a nice bamboo or wood hoop and some all-purpose glue. Place your piece in the hoop, making sure the piece is centered and it is nice and taut. Make sure the screw closure is centered as well, because that is what you are going to use to hang it. Trim the leftover fabric down to about 1 in (2.5 cm)—you want just enough to fold inside that bottom hoop. Draw a thin line of glue around the inside of the bottom hoop, then press your leftover fabric border into the glue line.

Framing Your Piece

There are a lot of ways you can go here—from professional framing to just taping your piece to a board and putting it in a frame. If you're using a photo frame, the easiest way is to trim your piece, leaving about 1 inch (2.5 cm) of border, place it in the frame, insert the back of the frame so the border hangs over the side, then tack down the border to the back of the frame (or don't—it's the back of the piece, so who's going to see it?).

If you're worried about wrinkles, a great alternative is to use self-adhesive mounting board. This board has one side with a strong adhesive; just cut it to the size you need (if you're putting it in a frame, use the back of the frame as your guide), peel off the sticky side, and place your piece on it (you can lift it up and rearrange as much as you like). Press down to smooth out any wrinkles, then place it in the frame.

JOY, JOY, JOY!

The beauty of cross-stitch is that there really isn't a wrong way to do it—no wrong way to hold your hoop, work a pattern, or even mount your piece. If you find a way of stitching that works better than how we have described it here, go for it! If you want to knot your floss or use a frame rather than a hoop, why not? A friend got so stressed out about the back of her piece not being perfect because her mom said that was "the rule" that she couldn't even get started. But there are no rules. Do what works for you. Once you start stitching, you'll find your own pace and your own style—and the inner fucking peace that can come from stabbing something lots and lots of times.

HAVE FUN!

THE PATTERNS

MERRY CHRYSLER

Sometimes spitting out those greetings is hard.

COLOR BLOCK	FLOSS NUMBER	COLOR NAME	STITCHES	STRANDS	SKEINS
∞	498	Dark Red	58	2	1
⠆	666	Bright Red	493	2	1
⊙	813	Light Blue	105	2	1
△	827	Very Light Blue	53	2	1
⬭	909	Very Dark Emerald Green	49	2	1
⌘	911	Medium Emerald Green	468	2	1
●	3822	Light Straw	75	2	1

PATTERN INFORMATION

Fabric: 14-count light-colored Aida, 11 × 11 in (28 × 28 cm)
Needle Size: 24
Stitch Count: 90 × 88
Finished Size: 6 × 6 in (5 × 5 cm)
Mounting: 8 or 9 in (20 or 23 cm) hoop

SIZE VARIATIONS

12-count Aida: 7.5 × 7 in (19 × 18 cm)
16-count Aida: 5.5 × 5.5 in (14 × 14 cm)
18-count Aida: 5 × 5 in (13 × 13 cm)

Design by
STITCHED CAT

COLOR BLOCK	FLOSS NUMBER
∞	498
∴	666
⊙	813
△	827
⬭	909
⌘	911
●	3822

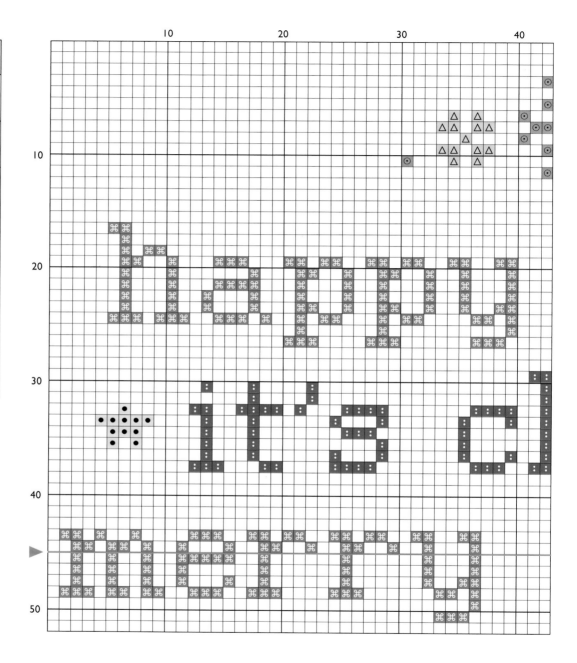

COLOR BLOCK	FLOSS NUMBER
∞	498
⠿	666
⊙	813
△	827
⬭	909
⌘	911
●	3822

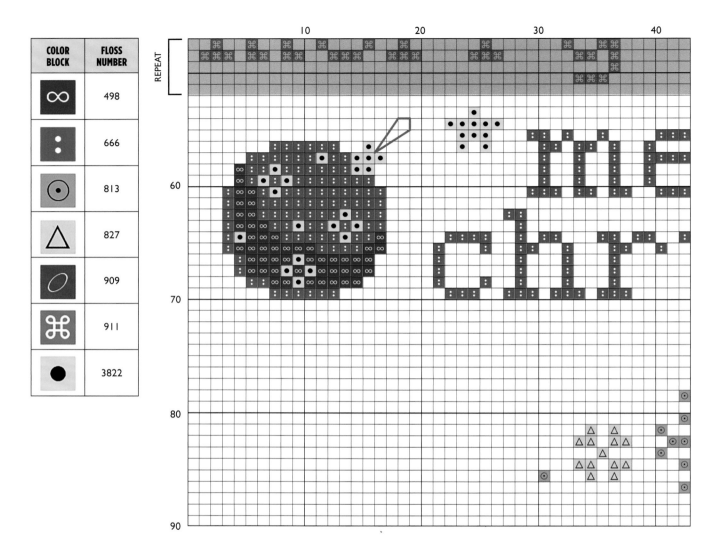

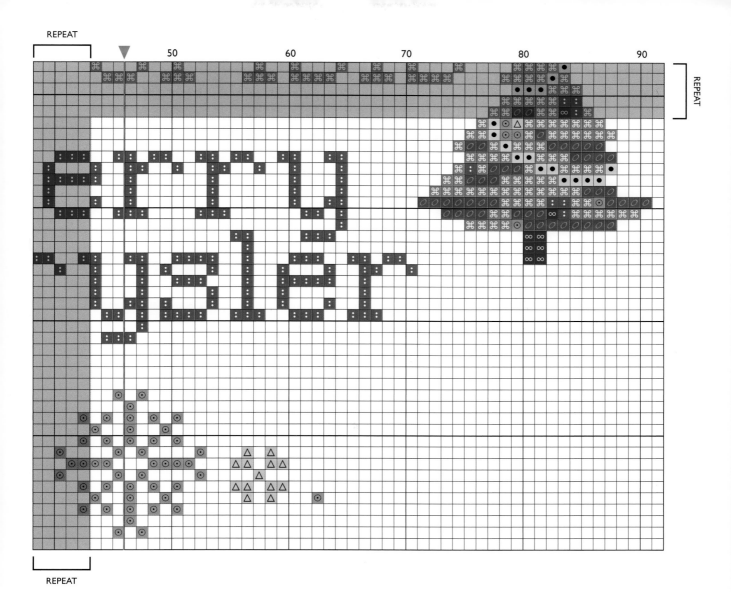

REPEAT

50   60   70   80   90

REPEAT

REPEAT

HO CHRISTMAS BAUBLE

When you want to shorthand the cheer.

COLOR BLOCK	FLOSS NUMBER	COLOR NAME	STITCHES	STRANDS	SKEINS
	666	Bright Red	220	2	1
	700	Bright Green	150	2	1

PATTERN INFORMATION

Fabric: 14-count white Aida, 9 × 9 in (23 × 23 cm)
Needle Size: 24
Stitch Count: 47 × 41
Finished Size: 3.5 × 3 in (9 × 7.5 cm)
Mounting: 3 or 4 (7.5 or 10 cm) in hoop

SIZE VARIATIONS

12-count Aida: 4 × 3.5 in (10 × 9 cm)
16-count Aida: 3 × 2.5 in (7.5 × 6 cm)
18-count Aida: 2.5 × 2 in (6 × 5 cm)

Design by **CURIOUS TWIST**

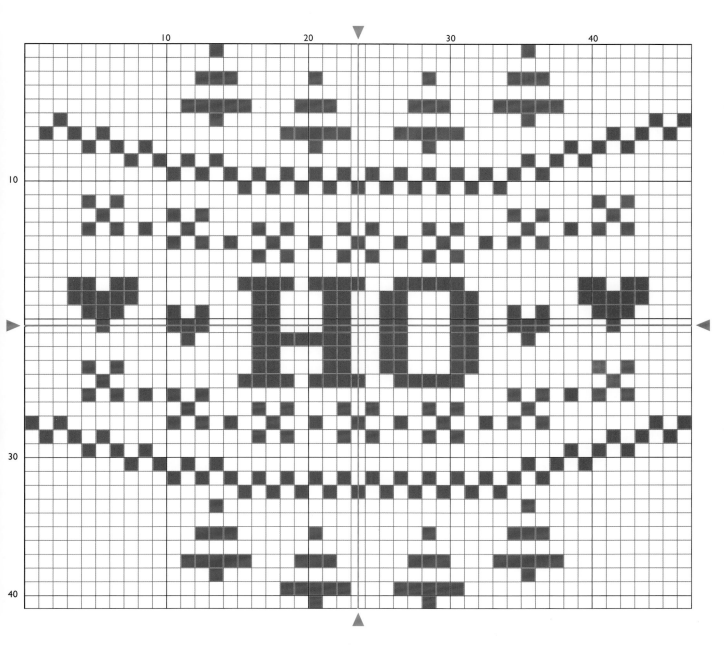

FESTIVE AF

When you're the holliest-jolliest, and you want them to know it.

COLOR BLOCK	FLOSS NUMBER	COLOR NAME	STITCHES	STRANDS	SKEINS
Ø	BLANC	White	2	2	1
■	310	Black	25	2	1
Ω	321	Red	159	2	1
✕	434	Light Brown	120	2	1
▪	435	Very Light Brown	197	2	1
●	606	Bright Orange Red	514	2	1
⌘	702	Kelly Green	280	2	1
△	738	Very Light Tan	178	2	1
◇	3818	Ultra Very Dark Emerald Green	278	2	1

PATTERN INFORMATION

Fabric: 14-count white Aida, 10 × 12 in (25 × 30.5 cm)
Needle Size: 24
Stitch Count: 61 × 88
Finished Size: 4 × 6 in (10 × 15 cm)
Mounting: 5 × 7 (13 × 18 cm) in frame

SIZE VARIATIONS

12-count Aida: 5 × 7 in (13 × 18 cm)
16-count Aida: 4 × 5.5 in (10 × 14 cm)
18-count Aida: 3 × 4 in (7.5 × 10 cm)

Design by **THE STRANDED STITCH**

COLOR BLOCK	FLOSS NUMBER
⌀	BLANC
■	310
Ω	321
✕	434
■	435
●	606
⌘	702
△	738
◇	3818

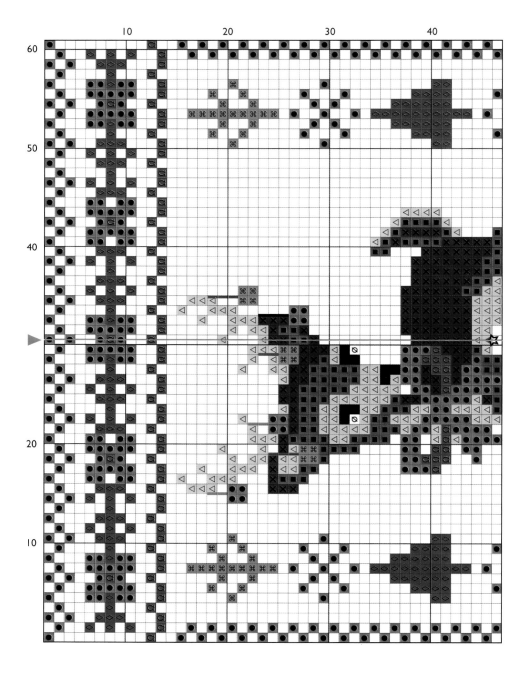

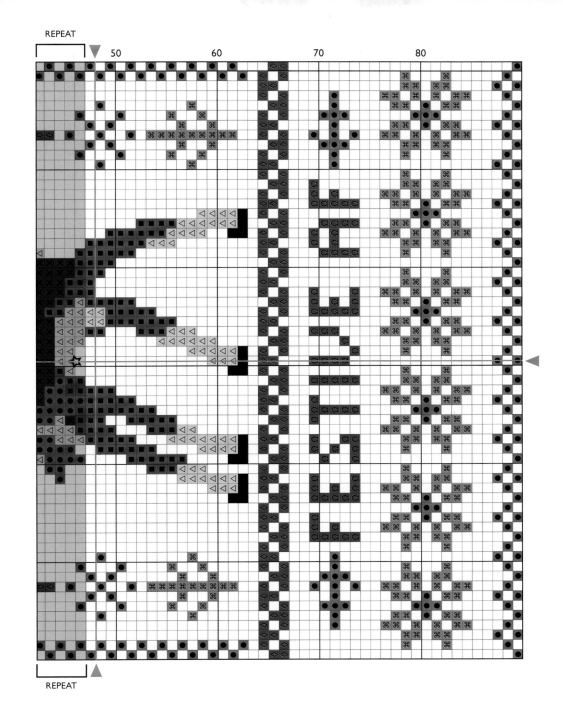

FANCY HOLIDAY ANXIℇTY

Deck your stress with boughs of holly ...

COLOR BLOCK	FLOSS NUMBER	COLOR NAME	STITCHES	STRANDS	SKEINS
♥	321	Red	630	2	0.3
⚕	322	Dark Baby Blue	522	2	0.2
✳	597	Turquoise	41	2	0.1
▲	699	Green	99	2	0.1
♣	701	Light Green	137	2	0.1
★	B5200	Snow White	161	2	0.1
BACKSTITCH					
——	310	Black	2.29 in (5.8 cm)	2	0.1
——	321	Red	41.60 in (105.7 cm)	2	0.3
——	597	Turquoise	4.15 in (10.5 cm)	2	0.1
——	701	Light Green	2.61 in (6.6 cm)	2	0.1

PATTERN INFORMATION

Fabric: 14-count white Aida, 13 × 13 in (33 × 33 cm)
Needle Size: 24
Stitch Count: 94 × 93
Finished Size: 6.75 × 6.75 in (17 × 17 cm)
Mounting: 8 in (17 × 17 cm) hoop

SIZE VARIATIONS

12-count Aida: 8 × 8 in (20 × 20 cm)
14-count Aida: 7 × 7 in (18 × 18 cm)
16-count Aida: 6 × 6 in (15 × 15 cm)

Design by
AMYLEE OF KIXSTITCHES

COLOR BLOCK	FLOSS NUMBER
♥	321
ℓ	322
✳	597
▲	699
♣	701
★	B5200
BACKSTITCH	
——	310
——	321
——	597
——	701

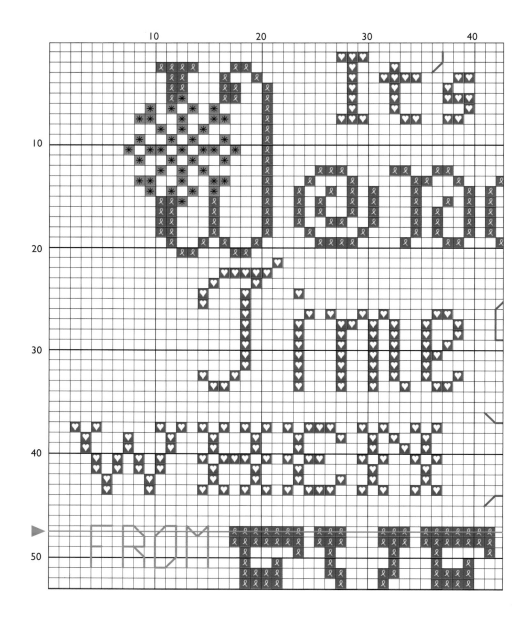

COLOR BLOCK	FLOSS NUMBER
♥	321
℘	322
✳	597
▲	699
♣	701
★	B5200
BACKSTITCH	
———	310
———	321
———	597
———	701

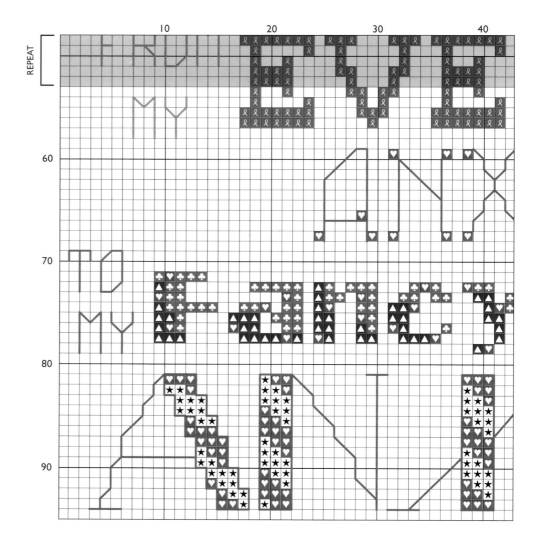

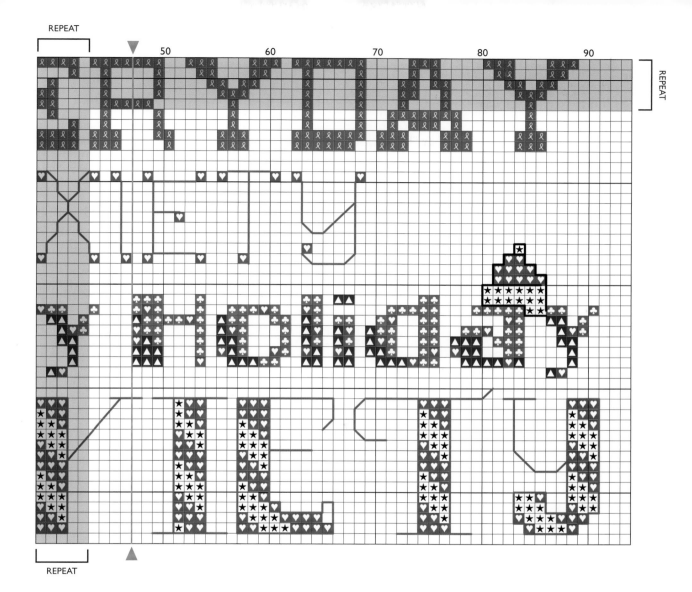

HAPPY HOLIDAZe

Taking the holidays one toke at a time.

COLOR BLOCK	FLOSS NUMBER	COLOR NAME	STITCHES	STRANDS	SKEINS
★	320	Medium Pistachio Green	632	2	0.3
♥	321	Red	1044	2	0.4
◈	699	Green	1052	2	0.4

PATTERN INFORMATION

Fabric: 14-count white Aida, 15 × 13 in (38 × 33 cm)
Needle Size: 24
Stitch Count: 118 × 100
Finished Size: 8.5 × 7 in (21.5 × 18 cm)
Mounting: 8 × 10 in (20 × 25 cm) frame or 10 in (25 cm) hoop

SIZE VARIATIONS

12-count Aida: 10 × 8 in (25 × 20 cm)
16-count Aida: 7.5 × 6 in (19 × 15 cm)
18-count Aida: 6.5 × 5.5 in (16.5 × 14 cm)

Design by
AMYLEE OF KIXSTITCHES

COLOR BLOCK	FLOSS NUMBER
★	320
♥	321
◈	699

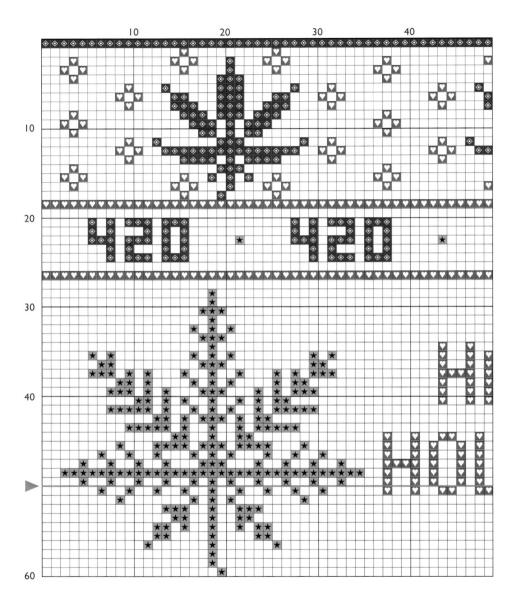

COLOR BLOCK	FLOSS NUMBER
★	320
♥	321
◈	699

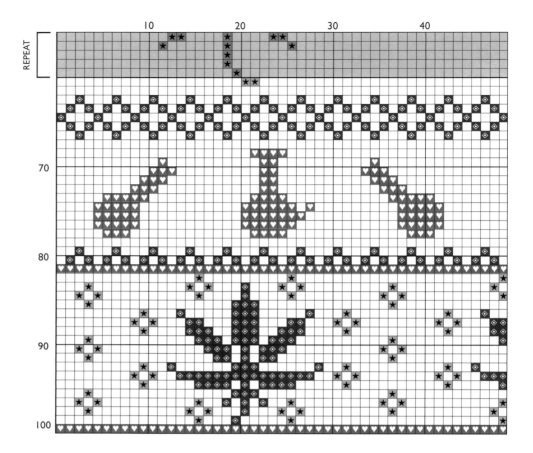

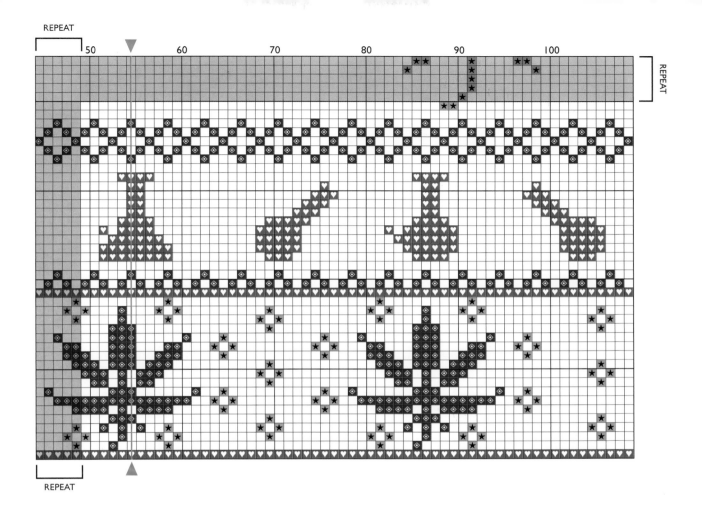

MERRY DRUNK, I'M CHRISTMAS

Getting into the holiday spirit ... and the spirits.

COLOR BLOCK	FLOSS NUMBER	COLOR NAME	STITCHES	STRANDS	SKEINS
■	321	Red	612	2	1

PATTERN INFORMATION

Fabric: 14-count cream Aida, 10 × 10 in (25 × 25 cm)
Needle Size: 24
Stitch Count: 50 × 50
Finished Size: 4 × 4 in (10 × 10 cm)
Mounting: 4 in (10 cm) hoop

SIZE VARIATIONS

12-count Aida: 4 × 4 in (10 × 10 cm)
16-count Aida: 3 × 3 in (7.5 × 7.5 cm)
18-count Aida: 2.75 × 2.75 in (7 × 7 cm)

Design by
BEVERLY ELLIS

Dasher, Dancer, Prancer, Vixen, Whiskey, Vodka, Tequila & Blitzen

ADULT REINDEER GAMES

No wonder Rudolph's nose was red.

COLOR BLOCK	FLOSS NUMBER	COLOR NAME	STITCHES	STRANDS	SKEINS
⠿	310	Black	942	2	1
❯	666	Bright Red	70	2	1
▣	700	Bright Green	32	2	1
▮	701	Light Green	16	2	1
=	729	Medium Old Gold	29	2	1
⌘	742	Light Tangerine	56	2	1
⊟	995	Dark Electric Blue	55	2	1
⬭	3829	Very Dark Old Gold	42	2	1
▮	3837	Ultra Dark Lavender	56	2	1
∫	B5200	Snow White	8	2	1

PATTERN INFORMATION

Fabric: 14-count white Aida, 12 × 12 in (25 × 25 cm)

Needle Size: 24

Stitch Count: 80 × 83

Finished Size: 6 × 6 in (15 × 15 cm)

Mounting: 8 × 8 in (20 × 20 cm) frame

SIZE VARIATIONS

12-count Aida: 7 × 7 in (18 × 18 cm)

16-count Aida: 5 × 5 in (13 × 13 cm)

18-count Aida: 4.5 × 5 in (11.5 × 13 cm)

Design by
ANGELA WALL

COLOR BLOCK	FLOSS NUMBER
∷	310
❯	666
▣	700
❘	701
═	729
⌘	742
⊟	995
⬮	3829
❙	3837
∽	B5200

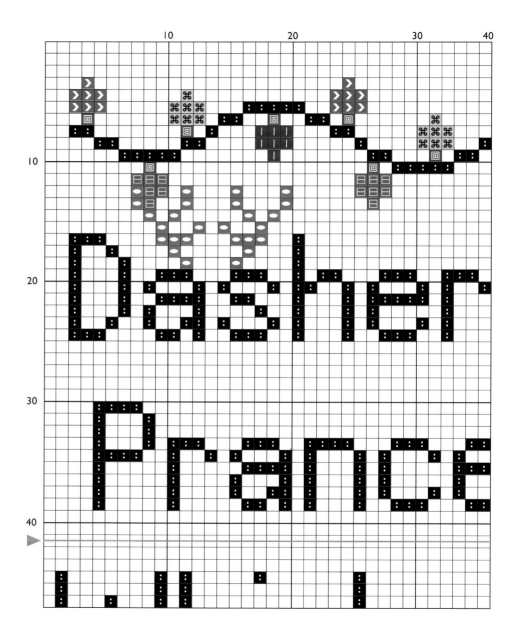

COLOR BLOCK	FLOSS NUMBER
⠿ (dots)	310
❯	666
▣	700
I	701
=	729
⌘	742
▤	995
⬭	3829
I	3837
ઽ	B5200

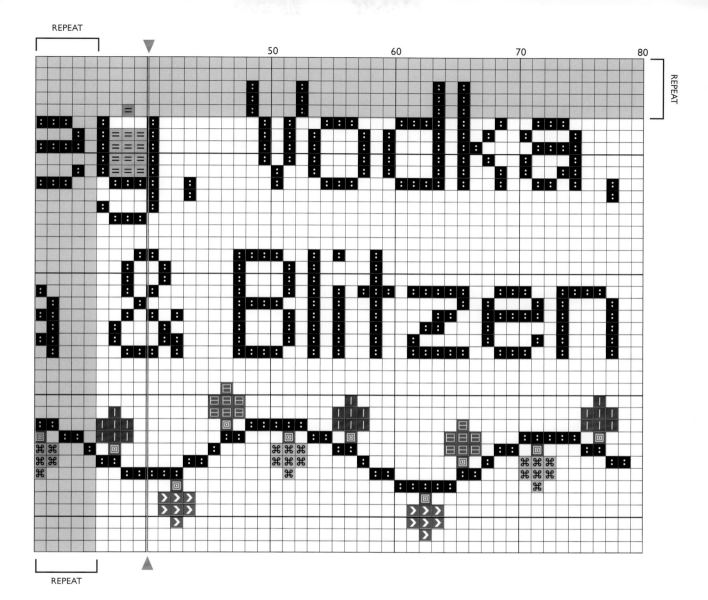

DECK THE HALLS AND NOT YOUR FAMILY

A cheerful reminder for the holiday family gatherings.

COLOR BLOCK	FLOSS NUMBER	COLOR NAME	STITCHES	STRANDS	SKEINS
⋮	310	Black	208	2 (back-stitch 1)	0.1
☘	666	Bright Red	342	2	0.3
4	700	Bright Green	483	2	0.3
C	Blanc	White	400	2	0.2

PATTERN INFORMATION

Fabric: 14-count beige Aida (or any color other than white, red, or green), 14 × 12 in (35.5 × 30.5 cm)
Needle Size: 24
Stitch Count: 111 × 78
Finished Size: 8 × 6 in (20 × 15 cm)
Mounting: 8 × 10 in (20 × 25 cm) frame

SIZE VARIATIONS

12-count Aida: 9 × 6.5 in (23 × 17 cm)
16-count Aida: 7 × 5 in (18 × 13 cm)
18-count Aida: 6 × 4 in (15 × 10 cm)

Design by
QUIRKY LITTLE STITCH CO.

COLOR BLOCK	FLOSS NUMBER
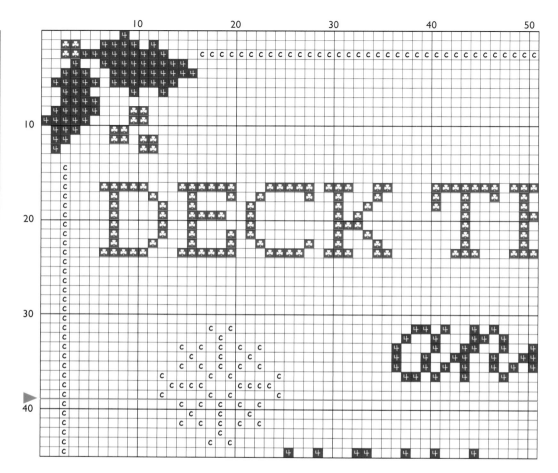	310
	666
	700
	Blanc

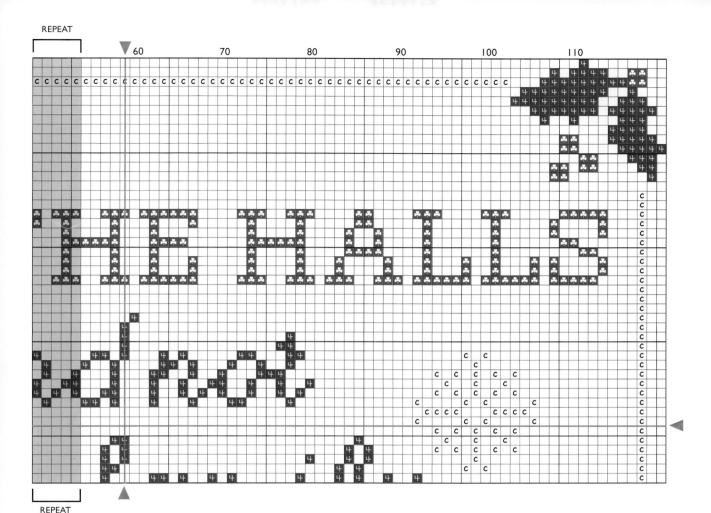

COLOR BLOCK	FLOSS NUMBER
⁘	310
♣	666
4	700
C	Blanc

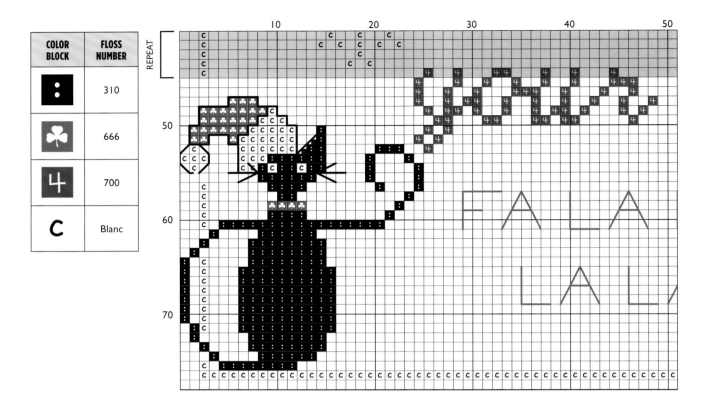

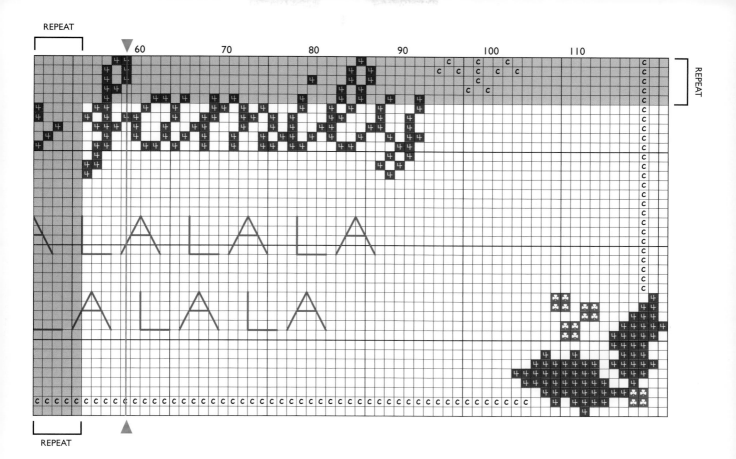

I LIKE YOUR BALLS

Celebrate those shiny danglers.

COLOR BLOCK	FLOSS NUMBER	COLOR NAME	STITCHES	STRANDS	SKEINS
	310	Black	19	2	1
	666	Bright Red	608	2	1.5
	820	Very Dark Royal Blue	299	2	1
	E168	Light Effects—Very Light Pewter	186	2	1
	E677	Light Effects—Very Light Old Gold	282	2	1
	E3821	Light Effects—Straw	479	2	1.5
	E3852	Light Effects—Very Dark Straw	187	2	1
	E5200	Light Effects—Snow White	160	2	1

PATTERN INFORMATION

Fabric: 14-count white Aida, 12 × 11 in (30.5 × 28 cm)
Needle Size: 24
Stitch Count: 90 × 65
Finished Size: 6 × 5 in (15 × 13 cm)
Mounting: 7 × 7 in (18 × 18 cm) frame or 8 in (20 cm) hoop

SIZE VARIATIONS

12-count Aida: 7.5 × 5 in (19 × 13 cm)
16-count Aida: 6 × 4 in (15 × 10 cm)
18-count Aida: 5 × 4 in (13 × 10 cm)

Design by
EMMA SNOW
LONDON CROSS
STITCH CLUB

COLOR BLOCK	FLOSS NUMBER
⋮	310
✚	666
✕	820
●	E168
◗	E677
✸	E3821
❙	E3852
i	E5200

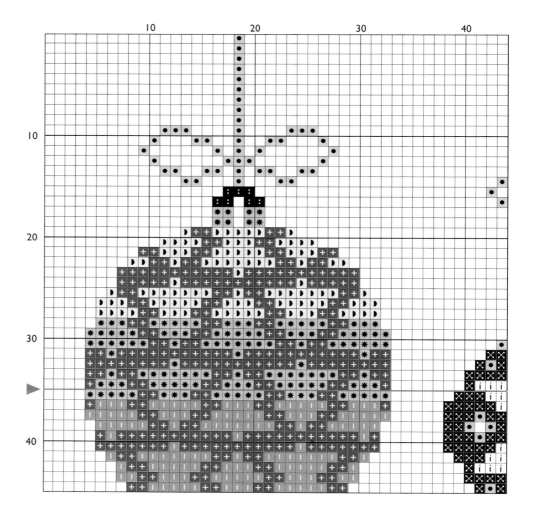

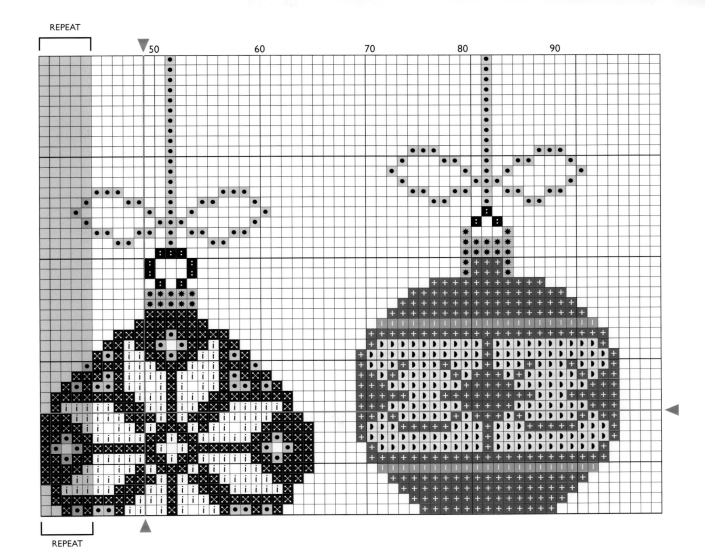

COLOR BLOCK	FLOSS NUMBER
⦂	310
+	666
✕	820
●	E168
◗	E677
✹	E3821
∣	E3852
i	E5200

When working with light effects DMC threads, work with a shorter amount because they get tangled very easily. Floss wax can be helpful here, but not essential. The finished effect is worth it! For the backstitching, use 2 strands of floss to make the baubles really pop! (See page 14 for backstitch instructions.)

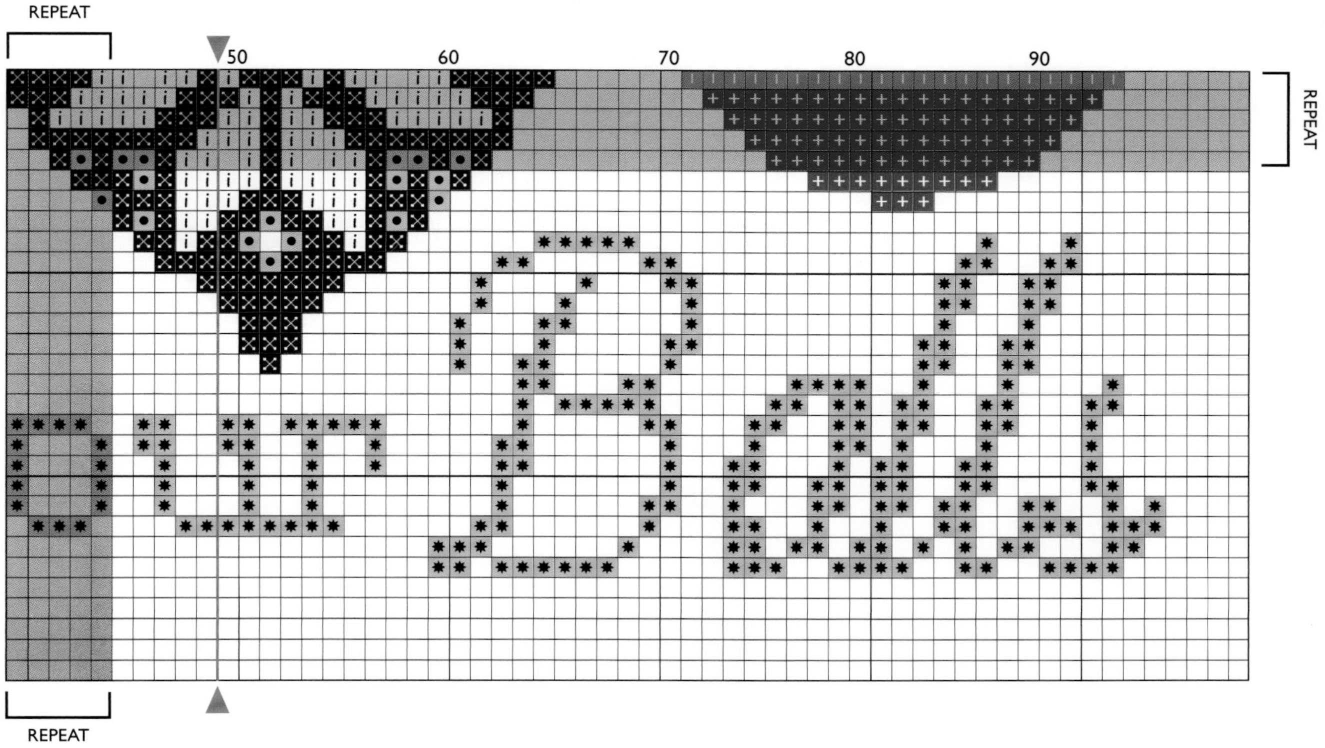
REPEAT
50
60
70
80
90
REPEAT
REPEAT

GANGSTA WRAPPER

A nod to the O.G. of present presentation.

COLOR BLOCK	FLOSS NUMBER	COLOR NAME	STITCHES	STRANDS	SKEINS
	159	Light Gray Blue	240	2	1
	160	Medium Gray Blue	406	2	1
	161	Gray Blue	370	2	1
	310	Black	619	2	2
	312	Very Dark Baby Blue	244	2	1
	351	Coral	72	2	1
	505	Jade Green	532	2	2
	550	Very Dark Violet	123	2	1
	553	Violet	144	2	1
	561	Very Dark Jade	106	2	1
	563	Light Jade	188	2	1
	606	Bright Orange-Red	110	2	1
§	704	Bright Chartreuse	99	2	1
W	725	Medium Light Topaz	494	2	1
	727	Very Light Topaz	32	2	1
	782	Dark Topaz	118	2	1
C	817	Very Dark Coral Red	154	2	1
Y	3810	Dark Turquoise	72	2	1

PATTERN INFORMATION

Fabric: 14-count white Aida, 13.5 x 15.5 in (34.5 x 40 cm)

Needle Size: 24

Stitch Count: 104 x 130

Finished Size: 7.5 x 9.5 in (19 x 24 cm)

Mounting: 8.5 x 11 in (21.5 x 28 cm) frame

SIZE VARIATIONS

12-count Aida: 9 x 11 in (23 x 28 cm)

16-count Aida: 6.5 x 8 in (16.5 x 20 cm)

18-count Aida: 6 x 7 in (15 x 18 cm)

Design by
JACLYN KOHLER

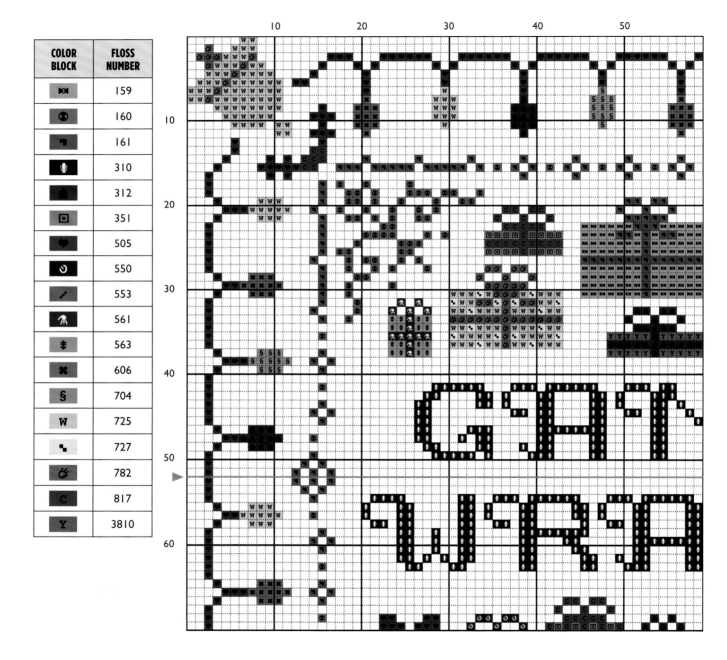

COLOR BLOCK	FLOSS NUMBER
	159
	160
	161
	310
	312
	351
	505
	550
	553
	561
	563
	606
S	704
W	725
	727
	782
C	817
Y	3810

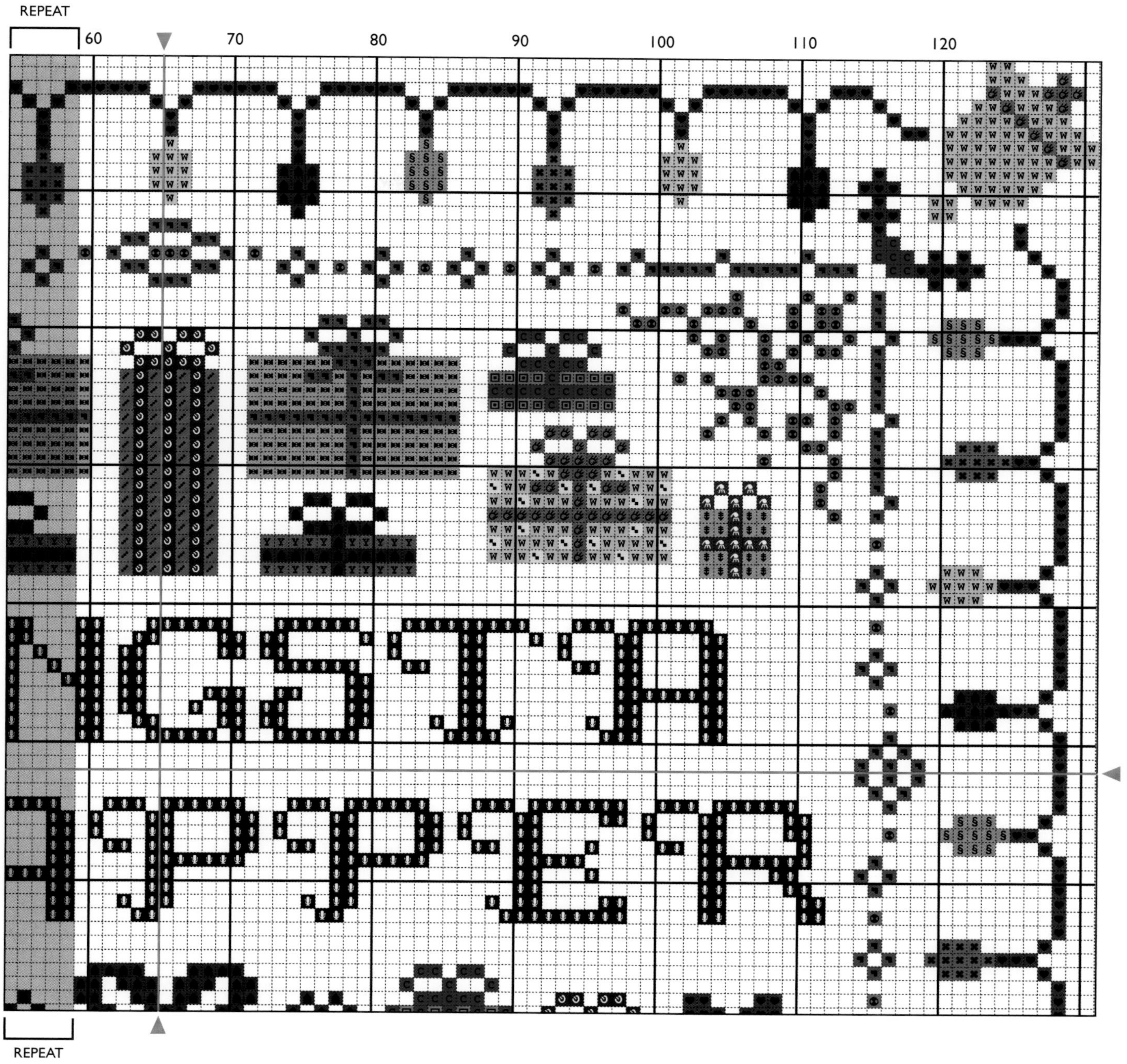
REPEAT
60
70
80
90
100
110
120
REPEAT

COLOR BLOCK	FLOSS NUMBER
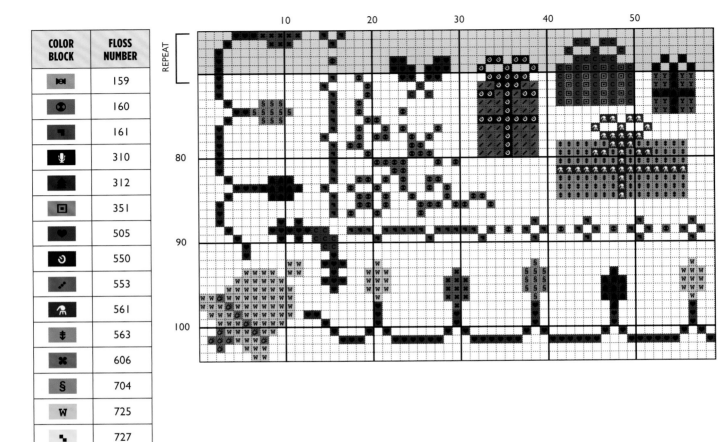 159

COLOR BLOCK	FLOSS NUMBER
▰	159
⊗	160
◣	161
♪	310
♠	312
▣	351
♥	505
↻	550
✦	553
♨	561
✚	563
✖	606
§	704
W	725
▪	727
✆	782
C	817
Y	3810

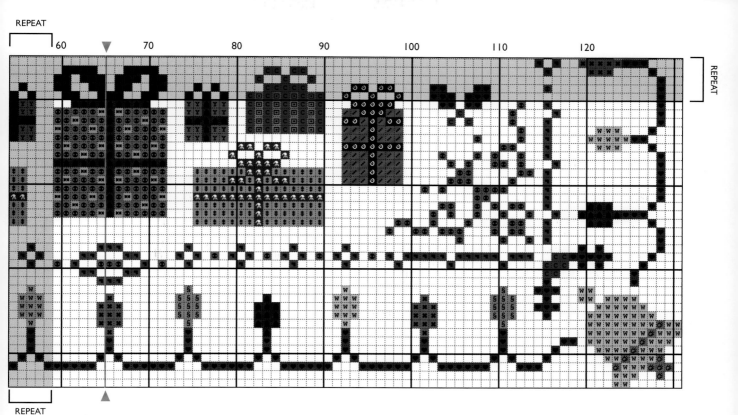

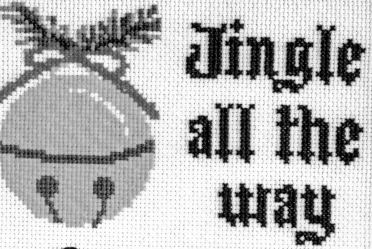

Jingle all the way

Nobody likes a
half-assed Jingler

JINGLE ALL THE WAY

Oh what fun it is to slay ... when you're the GOAT of the holidays.

COLOR BLOCK	FLOSS NUMBER	COLOR NAME	STITCHES	STRANDS	SKEINS
⊙	310	Black	627	2	1
✖	434	Light Brown	140	2	1
◖	444	Dark Lemon	859	2	1
✦	666	Bright Red	1722	2	1
//	699	Green	86	2	1
✳	703	Chartreuse	86	2	1
●	3799	Very Dark Pewter Grey	30	2	1
▲	B5200	Snow White	18	2	1

PATTERN INFORMATION

Fabric: 14-count white Aida, 12 × 12 in (30.5 × 30.5 cm)
Needle Size: 24
Stitch Count: 87 × 78
Finished Size: 6 × 6 in (15 × 15 cm)
Mounting: 8 × 8 in (20 × 20 cm) frame or 8 in (20 cm) hoop

SIZE VARIATIONS

12-count Aida: 7 × 6.5 in (18 × 16.5 cm)
16-count Aida: 5 × 5 in (12.5 × 12.5 cm)
18-count Aida: 5 × 4 in (12.5 × 10 cm)

Design by
SNARKY CRAFTER DESIGNS

COLOR BLOCK	FLOSS NUMBER
⊙	310
✖	434
⊖	444
✦	666
∥	699
✳	703
●	3799
↑	5200

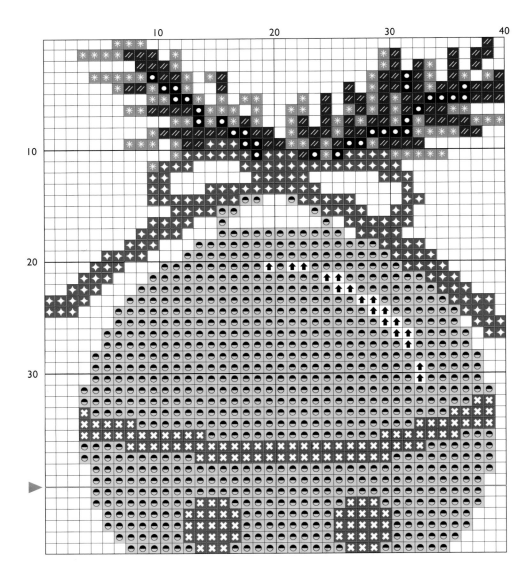

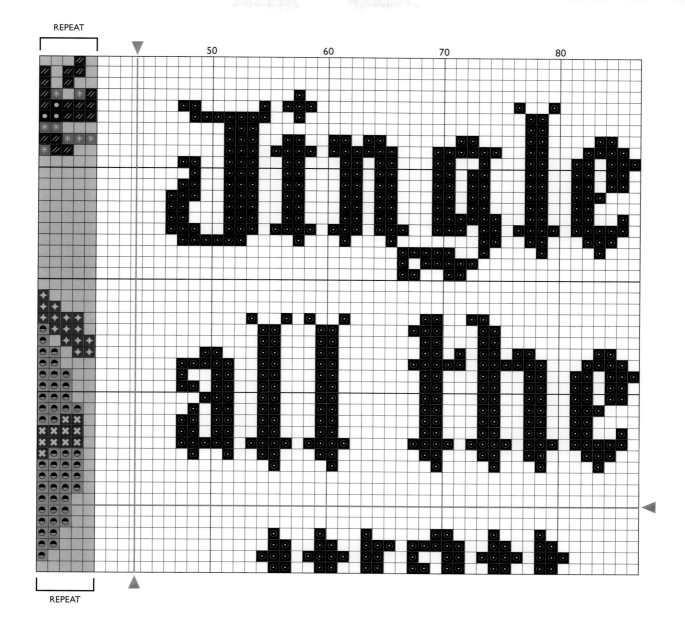

COLOR BLOCK	FLOSS NUMBER
⊙	310
✕	434
⊖	444
✦	666
//	699
✳	703
●	3799
↑	5200

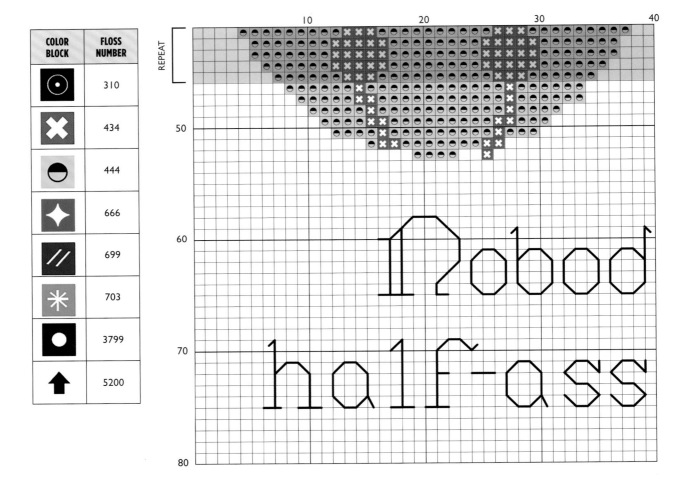

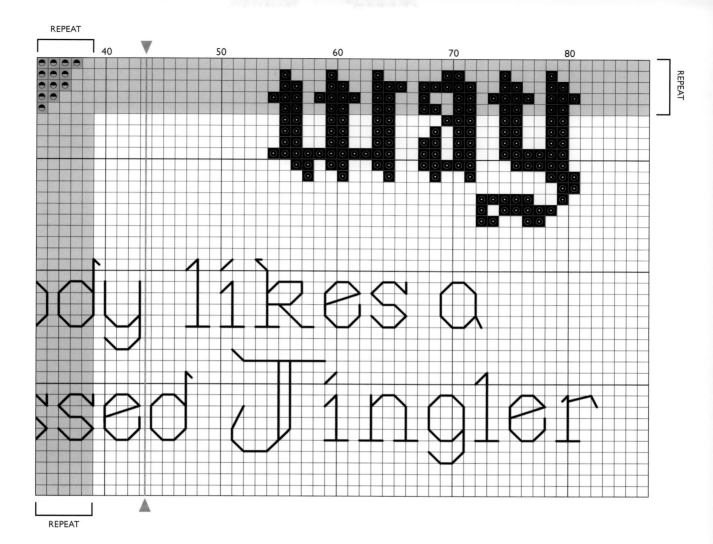

REPEAT

40   50   60   70   80

REPEAT

REPEAT

DIE HARD UGLY CHRISTMAS SWEATER

Merry Christmas, Argyle.

COLOR BLOCK	FLOSS NUMBER	COLOR NAME	STITCHES	STRANDS	SKEINS
	321	Red	284	2	1
	699	Green	609	2	2

PATTERN INFORMATION

Fabric: 14-count white or ivory Aida, 10 × 10 in (25 × 25 cm)
Needle Size: 24
Stitch Count: 57 × 58
Finished Size: 4 × 4 in (10 × 10 cm)
Mounting: 6 in (15 cm) hoop

SIZE VARIATIONS

12-count Aida: 5 × 5 in (12.5 × 12.5 cm)
16-count Aida: 3.5 × 3.5 in (9 × 9 cm)
18-count Aida: 3 × 3 in (7.5 × 7.5 cm)

Design by
PETER CAMERON

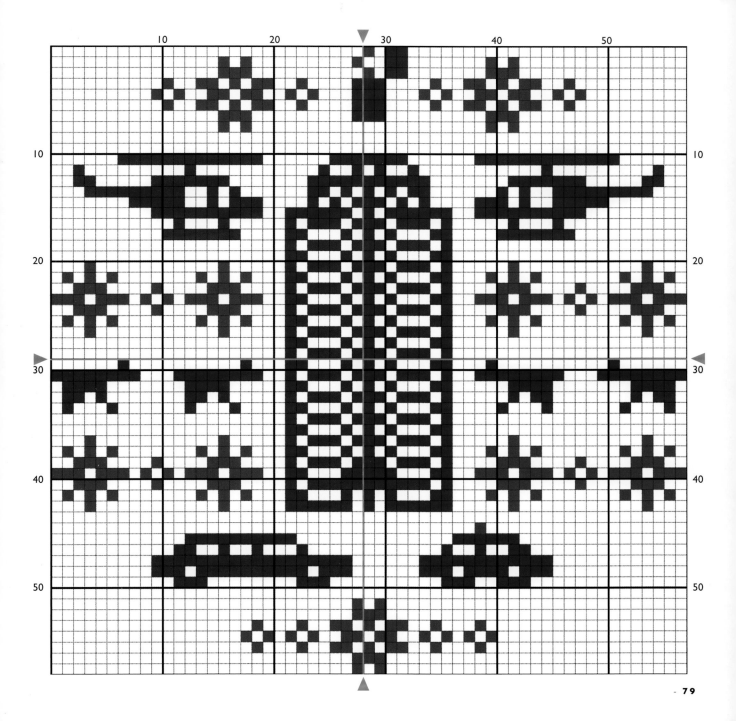

IT'S CHRISTMAS AND WE'RE ALL IN MISERY

If anyone knows about holiday misery, it's the Griswolds.

COLOR BLOCK	FLOSS NUMBER	COLOR NAME	STITCHES	STRANDS	SKEINS
≡	304	Medium Red	146	2	1
%	701	Light Green	48	2	1
♣	699	Green	680	2	1
♄	666	Bright Red	443	2	1

PATTERN INFORMATION

Fabric: 14-count white Aida, 12 × 12 in (30.5 × 30.5 cm)
Needle Size: 24
Stitch Count: 67 × 71
Finished Size: 6 × 6 in (15 × 15 cm)
Mounting: 7 in (18 cm) hoop

SIZE VARIATIONS

12-count Aida: 5.6 × 5.9 in (14 × 15 cm)
16-count Aida: 4 × 4 in (10 × 10 cm)
18-count Aida: 3 × 3 in (7.5 × 7.5 cm)

Design by
SNARKYSTITCHBITCH

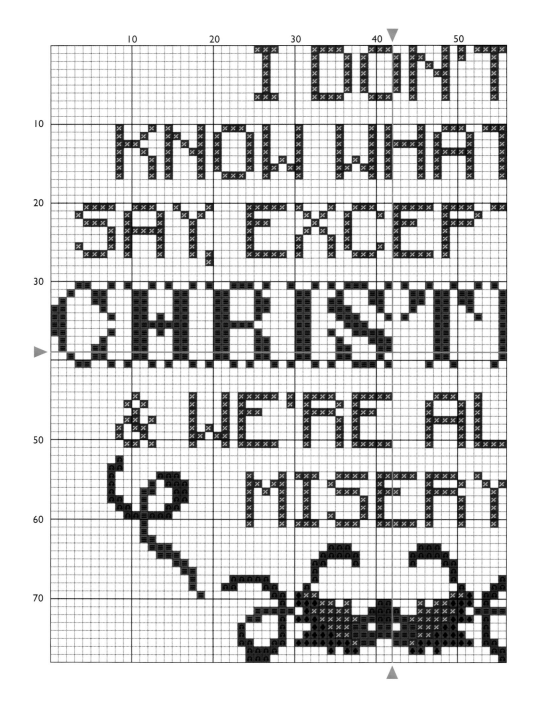

COLOR BLOCK	FLOSS NUMBER
≡	304
✕	701
♣	699
♫	666

REPEAT

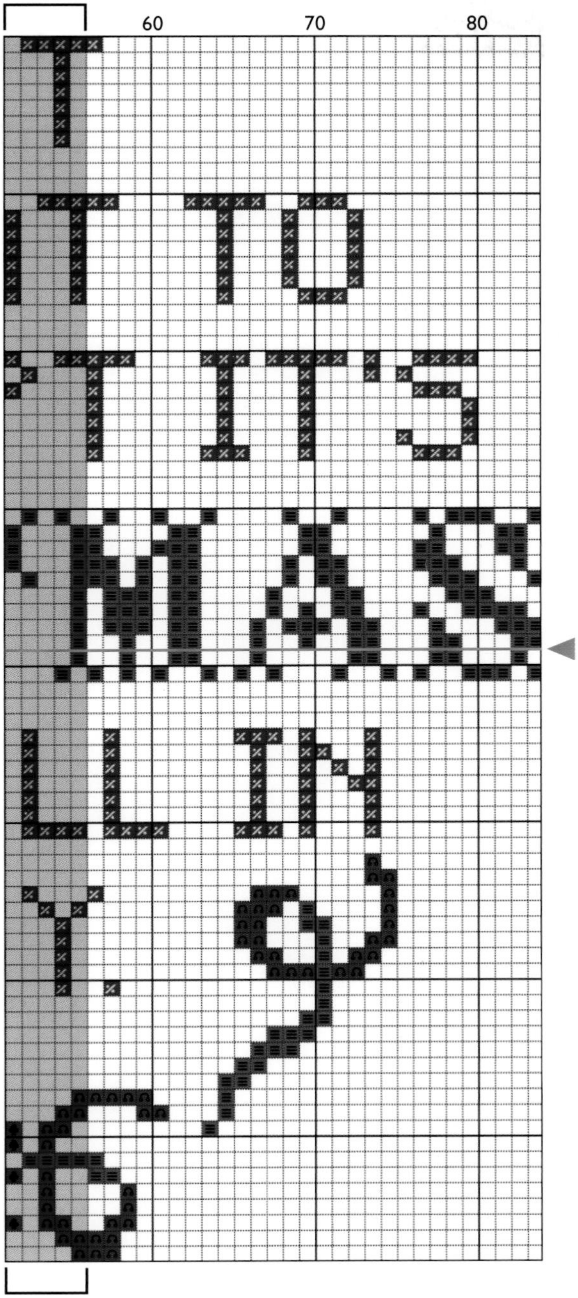

REPEAT

HALLELUJAH

HOLY SHIT

WHERE'S THE TYLENOL

HALLELUJAH, HOLY SHIT, WHERE'S THE TYLENOL?

The holidays summed up by Clark Griswold.

COLOR BLOCK	FLOSS NUMBER	COLOR NAME	STITCHES	STRANDS	SKEINS
●	BLANC	White	4203	2	3

This pattern features the last line of Clark's now-famous rant about his boss in *National Lampoon's Christmas Vacation*. Fun fact: That rant was almost completely ad-libbed by Chevy Chase. Cast members (with their backs to the camera) had signs around their necks, each with single-word prompts for Chevy—most of them were the adjectives he used to describe his cheap, lying, no-good, rotten, four-flushing boss.

PATTERN INFORMATION

Fabric: 14-count Christmas Green Aida, 14 × 16 in (35.5 × 40.5 cm)
Needle Size: 24
Stitch Count: 108 × 136
Finished Size: 8 × 10 in (20 × 25 cm)
Mounting: 8 × 10 in (20 × 25 cm) frame

SIZE VARIATIONS

12-count Aida: 9 × 11 in (23 × 28 cm)
16-count Aida: 7 × 8.5 in (18 × 21.5 cm)
18-count Aida: 6 × 7.5 in (15 × 19 cm)

Design by **BEVERLY ELLIS**

COLOR BLOCK	FLOSS NUMBER
●	BLANC

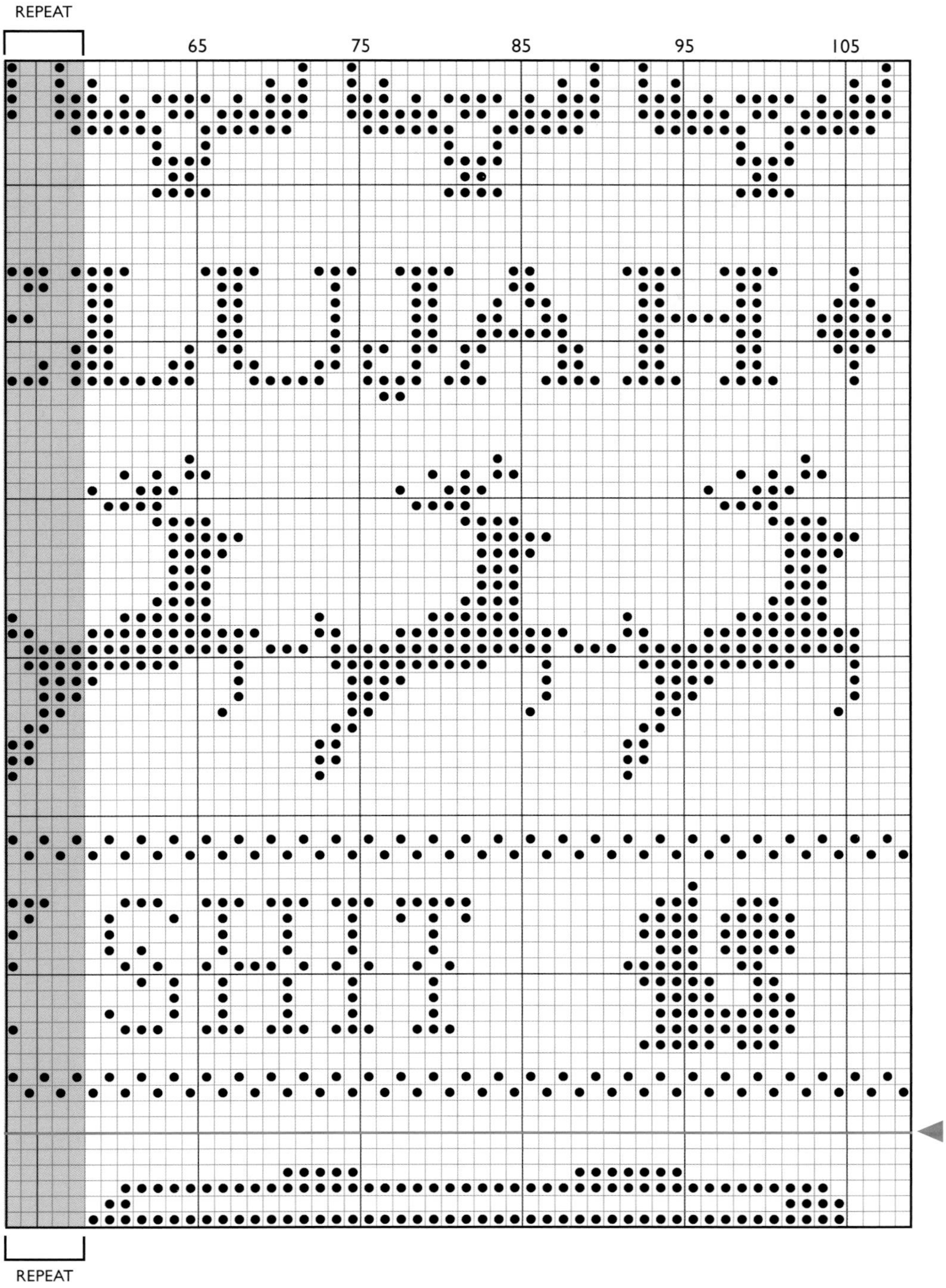
REPEAT
65
75
85
95
105
REPEAT

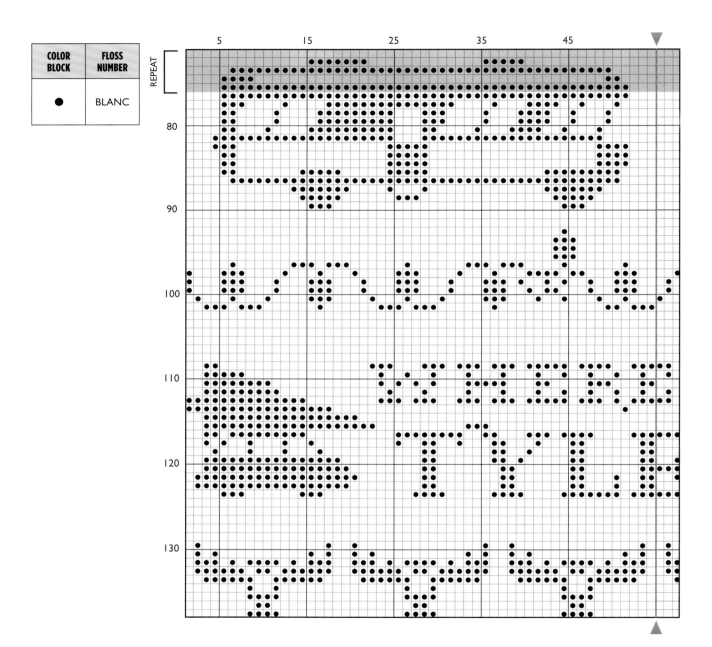

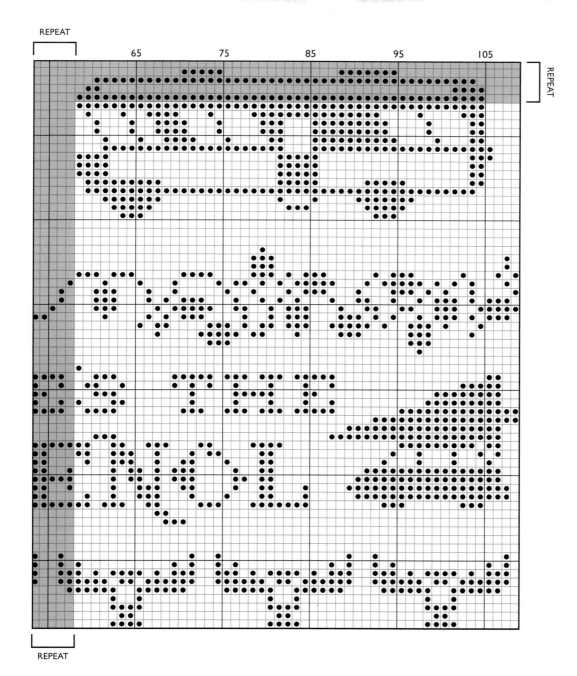

SNITCHES GET STITCHES

Word to the wise: don't piss off Jingle and Jangle.

COLOR BLOCK	FLOSS NUMBER	COLOR NAME	STITCHES	STRANDS	SKEINS
♥	168	Very Light Pewter	56	2	1
◖	304	Medium Red	432	2	1
▢	310	Black	693	2	1
◆	699	Green	464	2	1
◈	702	Kelly Green	503	2	1
✦	704	Bright Chartreuse	90	2	1
✳	729	Medium Old Gold	12	2	1
◑	814	Dark Garnet	224	2	1
⊙	3801	Very Dark Melon	85	2	1
✖	3829	Very Dark Old Gold	17	2	1
♡	BLANC	White	107	2	1

PATTERN INFORMATION

Fabric: 14-count ivory Aida, 12 × 12.5 in (30.5 × 32 cm)
Needle Size: 24
Stitch Count: 89 × 91
Finished Size: 6 × 6.5 in (15 × 16.5 cm)
Mounting: 7 or 8 in (18 or 20 cm) hoop

SIZE VARIATIONS

12-count Aida: 7.5 × 7.5 in (19 × 19 cm)
16-count Aida: 6 × 6 in (15 × 15 cm)
18-count Aida: 5 × 5 in (12.5 × 12.5 cm)

Design by
REBEKAH LEOTA
GAMEOVERSTITCHES

COLOR BLOCK	FLOSS NUMBER
♥	168
◐	304
□	310
◆	699
◈	702
✦	704
✳	729
◑	814
●	3801
✖	3829
♡	BLANC

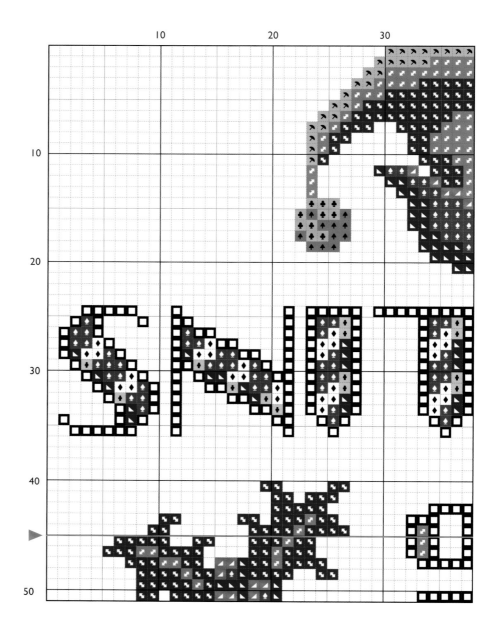

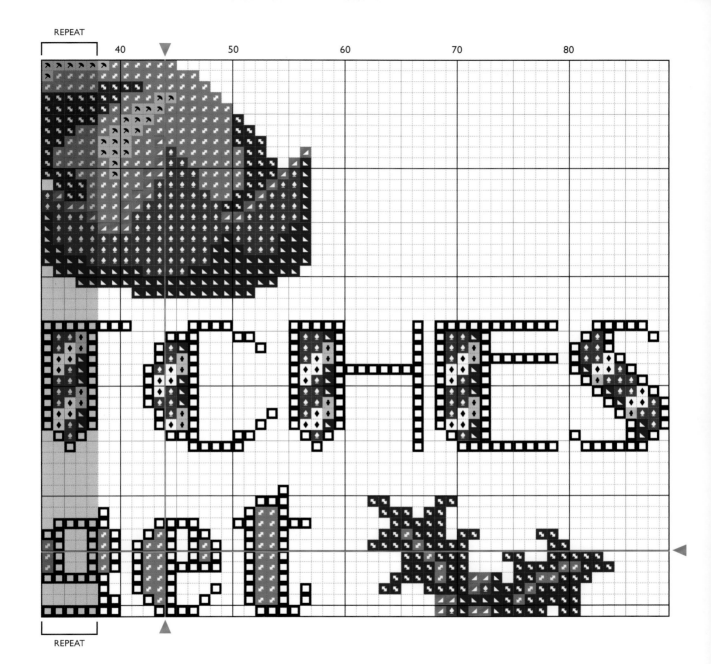

COLOR BLOCK	FLOSS NUMBER
♥	168
◑	304
☐	310
◆	699
◀▶	702
✦	704
✳	729
◧	814
⬤	3801
✖	3829
♡	BLANC

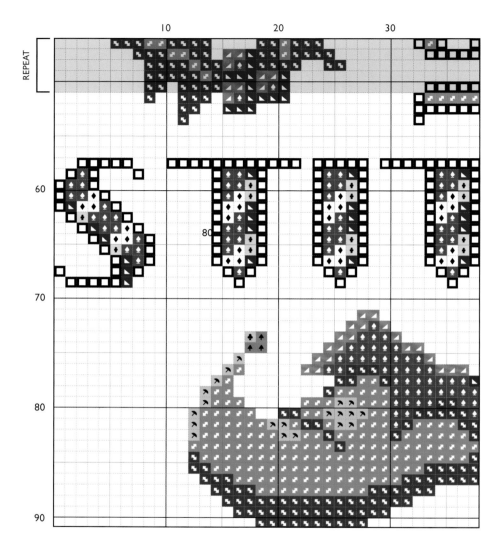

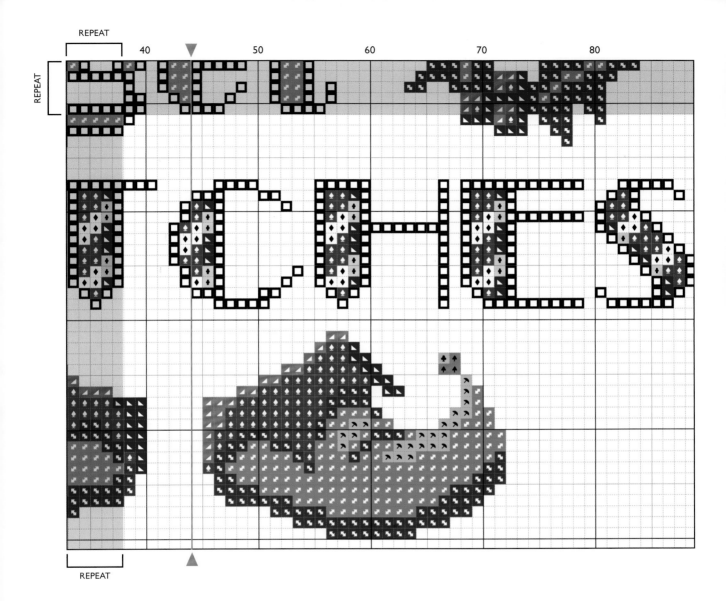

KRAMPUS

You've heard of elf on a shelf, now get ready for Krampus on a canvas.

COLOR BLOCK	FLOSS NUMBER	COLOR NAME	STITCHES	STRANDS	SKEINS
●	310	Black	1376	2	1
:-)	317	Pewter Gray	306	2	1
⌘	666	Bright Red	93	2	1
#	816	Garnet	321	2	1
⊠	987	Dark Forest Green	270	2	1
&	989	Forest Green	315	2	1
@	3012	Medium Khaki Green	423	2	1
✞	3031	Very Dark Mocha Brown	97	2	1
△	3046	Medium Yellow Beige	144	2	1
~	3799	Very Dark Pewter Gray	1233	2	1
✕	3865	Winter White	59	2	1

PATTERN INFORMATION

Fabric: 14-count light-colored Aida, 14 × 14 in (35.5 × 35.5 cm)
Needle Size: 24
Stitch Count: 113 × 107
Finished Size: 8 × 7.5 in (20 × 19 cm)
Mounting: 10 or 11 in (25 or 28 cm) hoop

SIZE VARIATIONS

12-count Aida: 9.5 × 9 in (24 × 23 cm)
16-count Aida: 7 × 7 in (18 × 18 cm)
18-count Aida: 6 × 6 in (15 × 15 cm)

Design by
STITCHED CAT

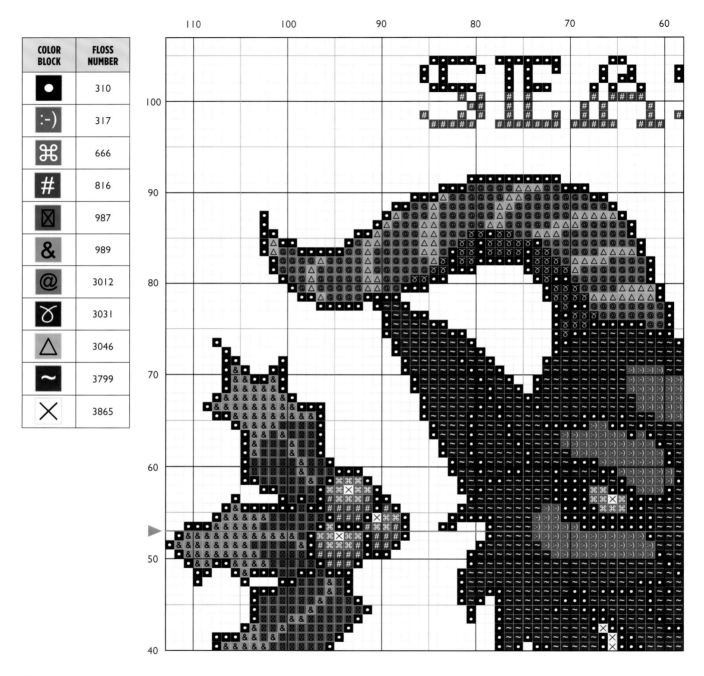

COLOR BLOCK	FLOSS NUMBER
●	310
:-)	317
⌘	666
#	816
⊠	987
&	989
@	3012
✗	3031
△	3046
~	3799
✕	3865

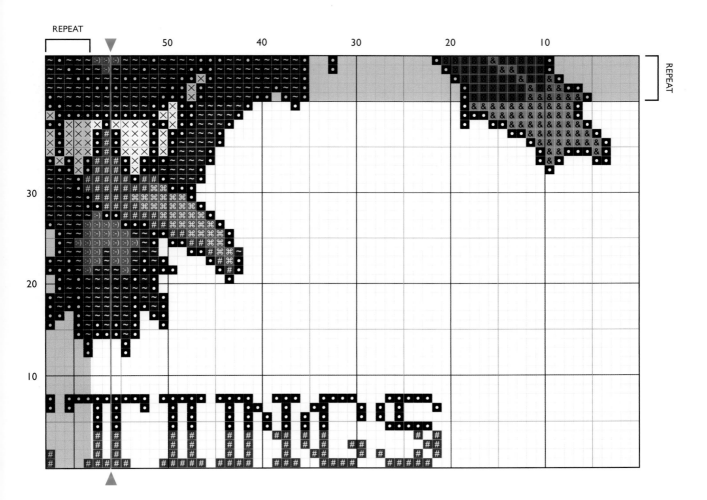

DEAR SANTA

Some things you just can't explain.

COLOR BLOCK	FLOSS NUMBER	COLOR NAME	STITCHES	STRANDS	SKEINS
◆	307	Lemon	73	2	0.1
⟱	310	Black	4470	2	2.1
♣	666	Bright Red	112	2	0.1
★	700	Bright Green	120	2	0.1
◣	824	Very Dark Blue	405	2	0.2

PATTERN INFORMATION

Fabric: 14-count white Aida, 18.5 x 23 in (47 x 58.5 cm)

Needle Size: 24

Stitch Count: 174 x 190

Finished Size: 12.5 x 17 in (32 x 43 cm)

Mounting: 14 x 18 in (35.5 x 46 cm) frame

SIZE VARIATIONS

12-count Aida: 14.5 x 16 in (37 x 41 cm)

16-count Aida: 11 x 12 in (28 x 30.5 cm)

18-count Aida: 10 x 11 in (25 x 28 cm)

Design by
K. E. HANN

COLOR BLOCK	FLOSS NUMBER
◆	307
☲	310
☘	666
★	700
◣	824

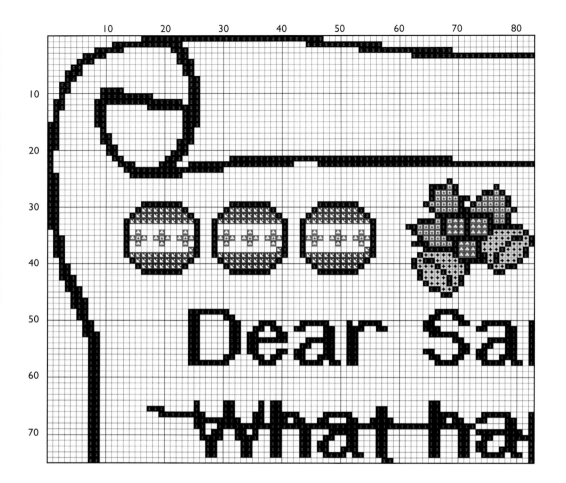

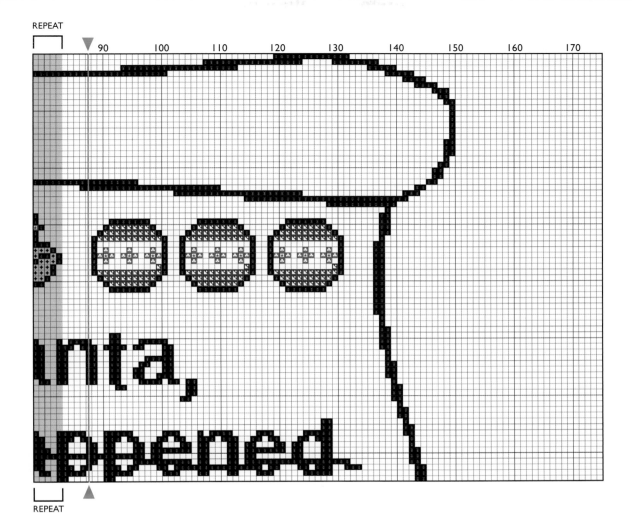

COLOR BLOCK	FLOSS NUMBER
◆	307
⟱	310
☘	666
★	700
◣	824

was

really

Fuck it, I

my own

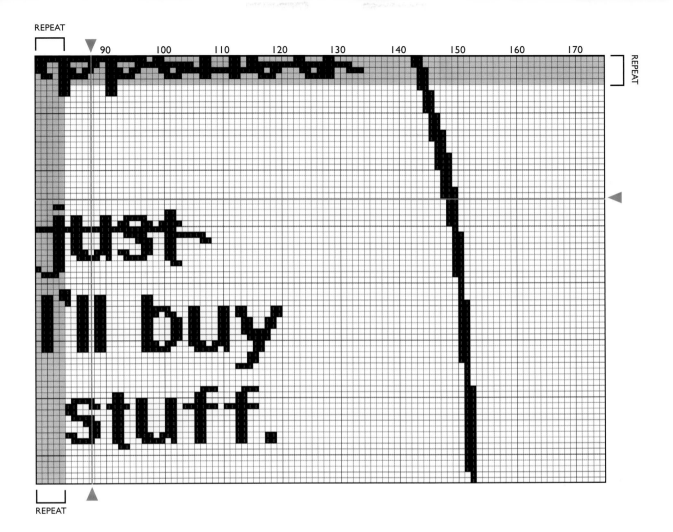

COLOR BLOCK	FLOSS NUMBER
◆	307
🌿	310
☘	666
★	700
◣	824

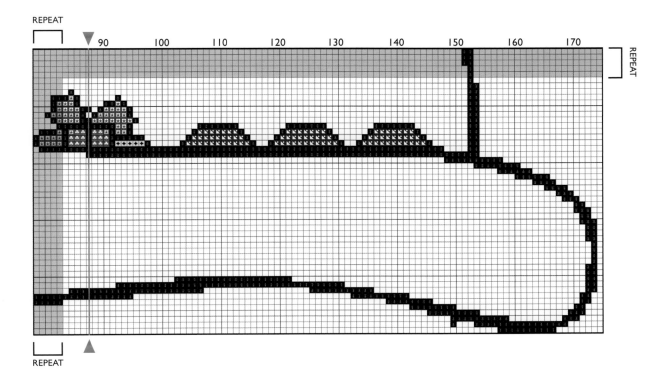

TWAƎ THE NIZZLE BEFORE CHRIƎTMIZZLE

The Christmas Eve classic, by way of Snoop.

COLOR BLOCK	FLOSS NUMBER	COLOR NAME	STITCHES	STRANDS	SKEINS
■	310	Black	49.8 in (126.5 cm) backstitch, 4 French knots	2	1
4	318	Light Steel Gray	29	2	1
5	415	Pearl Gray	441	2	1
·|·	434	Light Brown	14	2	1
=	469	Avocado Green	84	2	1
⅛	498	Dark Red	65	2	1
✚	720	Dark Orange Spice	214	2	1
◇	745	Light Pale Yellow	96	2	1
2	762	Very Light Pearl Gray	204	2	1
9	801	Dark Coffee Brown	94	2	1
⧁	814	Dark Garnet	46	2	1
▦	938	Ultra Dark Coffee Brown	1 stitch, 13 in (33 cm) backstitch	2	1
▼	3345	Dark Hunter Green	215	2	1
√	3826	Golden Brown	337	2	1
⊠	3834	Dark Grape	246	2	1
◩	3857	Dark Rosewood	154	2	1

PATTERN INFORMATION

Fabric: 14-count white Aida, 14 × 13 in (35.5 × 33 cm)

Needle Size: 24

Stitch Count: 105 × 91

Finished Size: 7.5 × 6.5 in (19 × 16.5 cm)

Mounting: 8 × 10 in (20 × 25 cm) frame

SIZE VARIATIONS

12-count Aida: 9 × 8 in (23 × 20 cm)

16-count Aida: 7 × 6 in (18 × 15 cm)

18-count Aida: 6 × 5 in (15 × 12.5 cm)

Design by **GABBY JEROME**

COLOR BLOCK	FLOSS NUMBER
■	310
4	318
5	415
•¦•	434
=	469
💀	498
✚	720
◇	745
2	762
9	801
⋘	814
▓	938
▼	3345
√	3826
⊠	3834
▨	3857

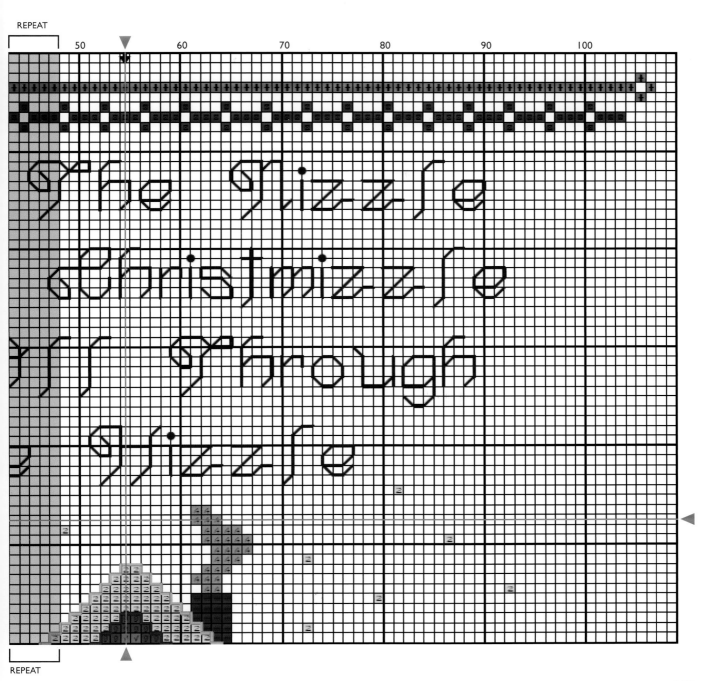

COLOR BLOCK	FLOSS NUMBER
■	310
4	318
5	415
·ǀ·	434
=	469
♣	498
✚	720
◇	745
2	762
9	801
⋘	814
⊞	938
▼	3345
√	3826
⊠	3834
◨	3857

REPEAT

There are three special stitches in this pattern. The first is the backstitch (see page 14 for instructions), the second is the French knot (see page 14), and the third is the quarter stitch, which is just a partial half stitch. To make it, pull the floss through the hole in the corner where the symbol sits (small symbol in the bottom right, start in the bottom right hole), then push the needle through the center of the cloth.

In the spots where the backstitch goes over multiple stitches, it's best to anchor it every two stitches to ensure it does not move. For the windowpanes, the artist suggests carrying the thread over all four stitches on the windowpane for this cabin because it is in the middle of the stitch row.

HO HO HOE

When you want to be a little naughty with your holiday cheer.

COLOR BLOCK	FLOSS NUMBER	COLOR NAME	STITCHES	STRANDS	SKEINS
◻	BLANC	Snow White	188	2	1
✶	702	Light Steel Gray	64	2	1
▷	890	Pearl Gray	32	2	1

PATTERN INFORMATION

Fabric: 14-count red Aida, 9 x 9 in (23 x 23 cm)
Needle Size: 24
Stitch Count: 45 x 39
Finished Size: 3 x 3 in (7.5 x 7.5 cm)
Mounting: 4 in (10 cm) hoop

SIZE VARIATIONS

12-count Aida: 4 x 3 in (10 x 7.5 cm)
16-count Aida: 3 x 2.5 in (7.5 x 6 cm)
18-count Aida: 2.5 x 2 in (6 x 5 cm)

Design by
STEPHANIE ROHR

116

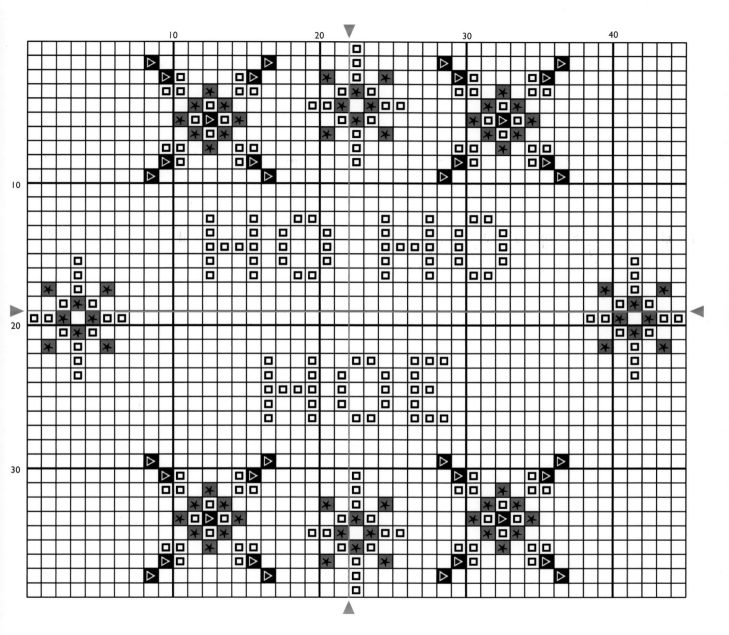

HAPPY FUCKING HOLIDAYS

Say it loud, for all to hear!

COLOR BLOCK	FLOSS NUMBER	COLOR NAME	STITCHES	STRANDS	SKEINS
	729	Old Gold Medium	1,338	3	2
	775	Baby Blue Very Light	509	3	1
	814	Garnet Dark	1,684	3	2
	890	Pistachio Green Ultra Dark	1,372	3	2

PATTERN INFORMATION

Fabric: 14-count white Aida, 14 × 14 in (35.5 × 35.5 cm)
Needle Size: 24
Stitch Count: 110 × 110
Finished Size: 8 × 8 in (20 × 20 cm)
Mounting: 9 × 9 in (23 × 23 cm) frame

SIZE VARIATIONS

12-count Aida: 9 × 9 in (23 × 23 cm)
16-count Aida: 7 × 7 in (18 × 18 cm)
18-count Aida: 6 × 6 in (15 × 15 cm)

Design by **AIMEE C. SAVEY**

COLOR BLOCK	FLOSS NUMBER
	729
	775
	814
	890

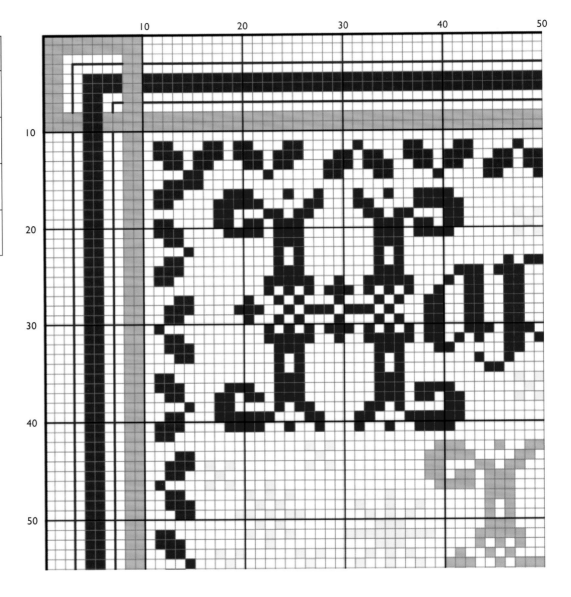

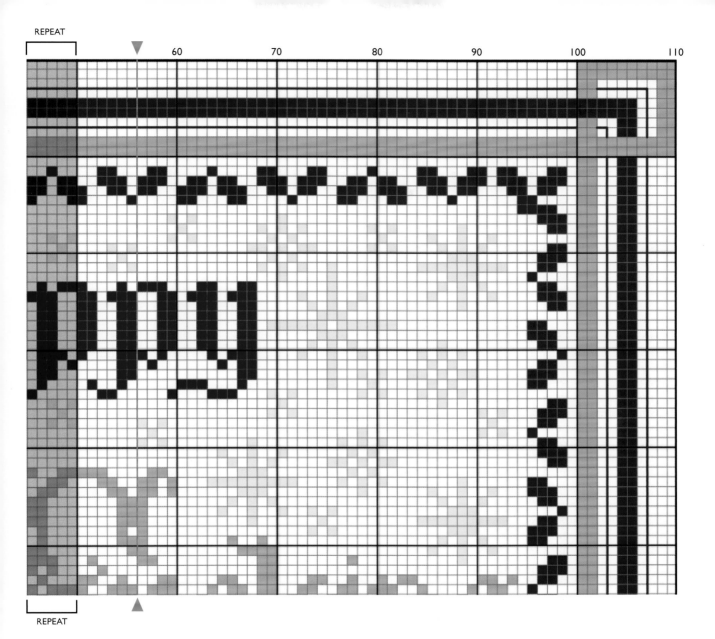

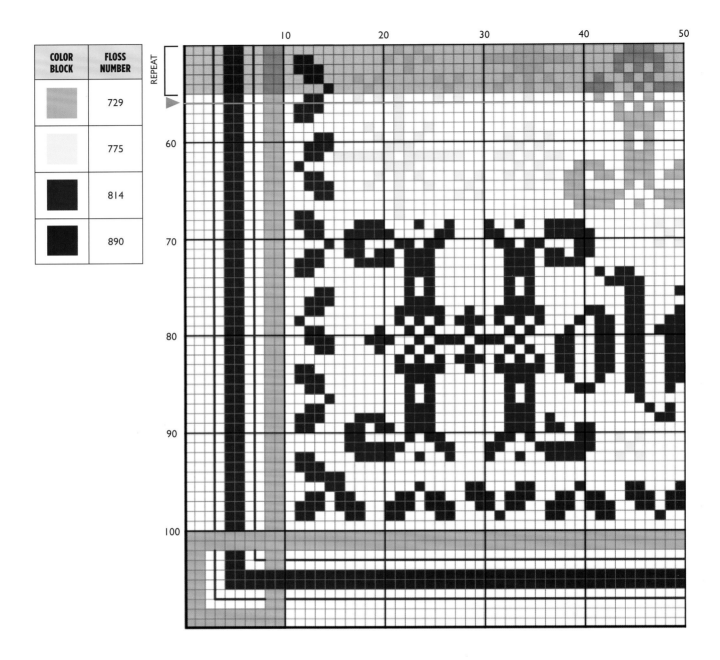

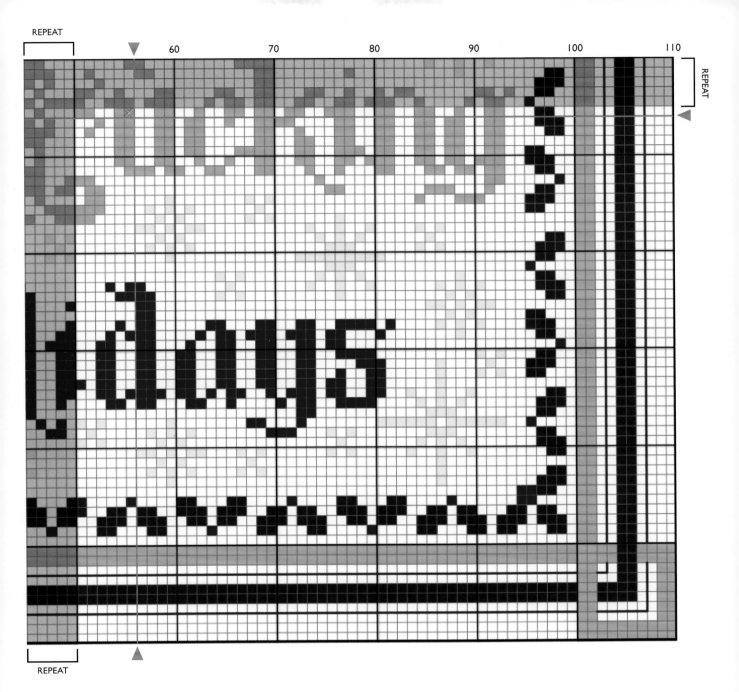

MEET THE ARTISTS

And now, a word about our artists—from the artists!

PETER CAMERON

Peter started to design cross-stitch patterns as a way to create something fun to share during the pandemic. As a huge fan of old video games, he loves cross-stitch as a medium for retro-inspired artwork and hopes to keep creating patterns that people love to make. If you would like to say hi, find him on Instagram @ghostrocketstudio.

CURIOUS TWIST

Curious Twist—cross-stitch for the classy, sassy, and totally badassy! To see more, visit www.curioustwist.com and follow us on Facebook @curioustwistshop, Instagram @curious.twist, and TikTok @curioustwist.

BEVERLY ELLIS

Beverly is a lifelong cross-stitcher, Christmas fanatic, and avid film buff. She makes patterns that are fun, easy, and accessible for stitchers of any skill level. You can find all her designs at etsy.com/shop/BeverlyStreetShop.

K. E. HANN

K. E. Hann started designing cross-stitch patterns as a form of CPTSD therapy. Quite quickly, she realized that being snarky was a great deal of fun and thus opened an Etsy shop to share her designs with the world. Presently, she is using her shop to raise money for various humanitarian and animal aid causes, most recently Ukraine. See more of her patterns at crankycatcrossstitch.etsy.com.

GABBY JEROME

For Gabby, cross-stitch started as a way to keep herself entertained when her children were little, and while her husband was busy with his military duties, but it opened the door to a whole new world of amazing communities and fantastic people. Gabby's goal with her shop, StitchyLittleFox, has always been to make people laugh. She creates patterns that are funny and puts them out into the world in the hopes that someone else finds them funny, too. To see more of Gabby's designs, visit StitchyLittleFox.com. Follow Gabby on Facebook at facebook.com/stitchylittlefox or Instagram @stitchylittlefox.

AMYLEE OF KIXSTITCHES

Born and raised in the suburbs of Chicago in the '90s, my home was filled with cross-stitches my grandfather created. They ranged from the typical cute pieces one would expect to see in any Midwestern home to many that had some unexpected dry humor stitched in. My grandfather's designs gave me a passion for cross-stitching that never left me and inspired me to create many of my own designs.

JACLYN KOHLER
Born and raised in New York, I grew up tearing through classic video games with my fellow clan of devoted nerds (a.k.a. my loving family). My Etsy shop displays a variation of patterns reflecting my unique sense of humor, but is mainly a collection of work built from self-care and warm childhood memories that I shared with my family. My Etsy shop can be located at www.jackthestitcher.etsy.com.

REBEKAH LEOTA (GAMEOVERSTITCHES)
Rebekah Leota started making patterns when she was looking for a cross-stitch project, but couldn't find anything that matched her personal taste and thought, "Why not do it myself?" After her first successful pattern, the ideas just kept coming faster than she had the time to actually stitch them, so she opened http://gameoverstitches.etsy.com to share her patterns with the public.

QUIRKY LITTLE STITCH CO.
Alison is the designer behind QuirkyLittleStitchCo. She has been a cross-stitcher for about twenty years and recently started designing her own quirky and fun patterns. Her aim is to create small patterns that can be completed over a weekend or two and give you a laugh! They're perfect to hang on your wall, sew on a cushion, or give as a gift! Visit her Etsy store at www.etsy.com/au/shop/QuirkyLittleStitchCo or follow her on Instagram @quirkylittlestitchco. Merry Christmas!

STEPHANIE ROHR
Stephanie Rohr is a Chicago-based cross-stitch designer who established her brand, stephXstitch, in 2010. She is the author of two pattern books: *Feminist Cross-Stitch* and *Self-Care Cross-Stitch*. You can find more of her work at stephXstitch.com and on Instagram, Facebook, Twitter, TikTok, Patreon, and Etsy @stephxstitch.

AIMEE C. SAVEY
Aimee C. Savey was an avid knitter before the pandemic, but after knitting nine sweaters back-to-back during quarantine, she turned to snarky cross-stitching to occupy that nervous energy at a fraction of the cost. She also likes tattoos and cats. Her patterns can be found at @EZBakedCrafts on Etsy.

SNARKY CRAFTER DESIGNS
Kim, the snarky creator behind Snarky Crafter Designs, specializes in original, sarcastic patterns and notions for cross-stitch and embroidery. With a husband, three kids, and two cats, she lives by the mantra "crafting is cheaper than therapy." You can find her on Facebook, Instagram, and Pinterest at @SnarkyCrafter or at her website: SnarkyCrafterDesigns.com.

SNARKYSTITCHBITCH

The SnarkyStitchBitch creates subversive, feminist, media-centric cross-stitch patterns as part of her effort to overthrow the patriarchy. Her alter ego, Rebecca Owen, is a mild-mannered librarian who loves cats, cheese fries, and rewatching her favorite movies. Find more of her patterns on her website, Snarkystitchbitch.com, or on Etsy at SnarkyStitchBitch.

EMMA SNOW OF LONDON CROSS STITCH CLUB

Emma is the owner of London Cross Stitch Club, which was started with an aim to make cross-stitch enticing to the next generation by providing easy and snarky patterns that everyone can enjoy. Classic samplers aren't the vibe here. You can find more patterns at londoncrossstitchclub.com. Emma does a happy dance every time she sees a finished piece—tag her @londoncrossstitchclub.

STITCHED CAT

Hello, my name is Nicole! I'm an illustrator by day and a stitcher by night. Around the beginning of the pandemic, I discovered cross-stitching and fell in love with the craft. Soon, I decided to try making my own patterns, inspired by internet memes and silly subversions, which led me to sharing them online. If you'd like, you can find more of my patterns on my Etsy at stitchedcat.etsy.com and follow my Instagram @stitched_cat for updates!

THE STRANDED STITCH

The Stranded Stitch is a Los Angeles–based cross-stitch pattern and kit company specializing in modern, beginner-friendly designs. You can find us online at www.thestrandedstitch.com.

ANGELA WALL

Nova Stitch Creations was established in 2018 by Angela Wall. Her cross-stitch patterns are inspired by her own unique blend of humor, words you "shouldn't" say in public, random fandoms, and an irreverent outlook on life. For more of Angela's work, you can find her at www.etsy.com/shop/novastitchcreations and follow her on Instagram @novastitchcreations.

weldonowen

an imprint of Insight Editions
P.O. Box 3088
San Rafael, CA 94912
www.weldonowen.com

CEO Raoul Goff
VP Publisher Roger Shaw
Editorial Director Katie Killebrew
Senior Editor Karyn Gerhard
VP Creative Chrissy Kwasnik
Art Director Allister Fein
Design Assistance Jean Hwang
VP Manufacturing Alix Nicholaeff
Sr Production Manager Joshua Smith
Sr Production Manager, Subsidiary Rights Lina s Palma-Temena

Photography of finished pieces by Jill Paice

Weldon Owen would also like to raise a glass of eggnog to the brilliant elves who helped in the creation of this slice of holiday cheer: proofreader Karen Levy; editorial assistant Jon Ellis; cross-stitcher Stacia Woodcock; photographer Jill Paice; and all of the cross-stitch artists whose fantastic pieces have made this book such a joy. Happy holidays!

Text © 2023 Weldon Owen International

ISBN: 979-8-88674-076-9

Manufactured in China by Insight Editions
10 9 8 7 6 5 4 3 2 1

ROOTS of PEACE   REPLANTED PAPER

Insight Editions, in association with Roots of Peace, will plant two trees for each tree used in the manufacturing of this book. Roots of Peace is an internationally renowned humanitarian organization dedicated to eradicating land mines worldwide and converting war-torn lands into productive farms and wildlife habitats. Roots of Peace will plant two million fruit and nut trees in Afghanistan and provide farmers there with the skills and support necessary for sustainable land use.

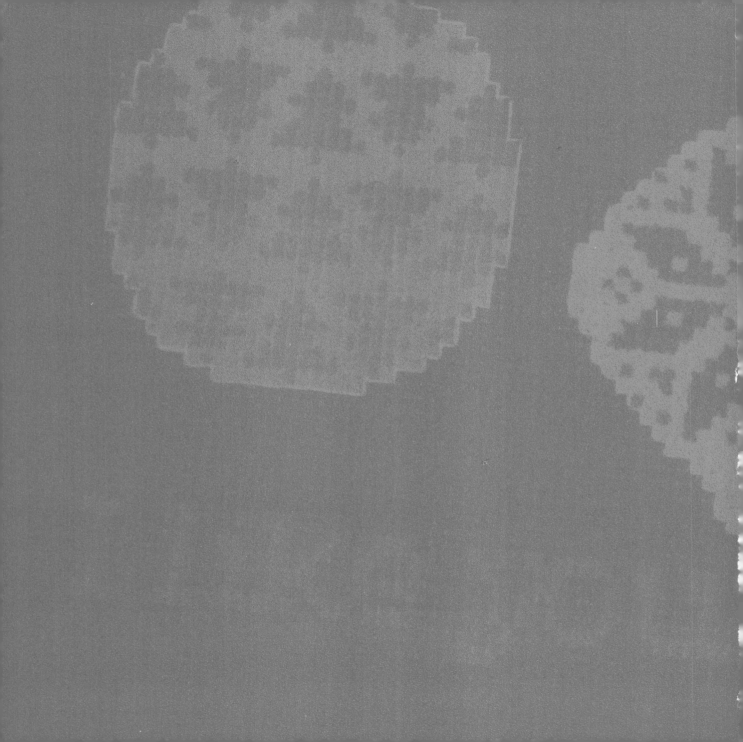